THE

RUNIC TAROT

THE
RUNIC TAROT

CAROLINE SMITH AND JOHN ASTROP

ST. MARTIN'S GRIFFIN
NEW YORK

Text and cards copyright © Caroline Smith and John Astrop 2003
This edition copyright © Eddison Sadd Editions 2003

Library of Congress Cataloging-in-Publication Data available on request.

ISBN 0-312-32192-9

First St. Martin's Griffin edition: 2003

1 3 5 7 9 10 8 6 4 2

AN EDDISON • SADD EDITION
Edited, designed and produced by
Eddison Sadd Editions Limited
St Chad's House, 148 King's Cross Road
London WC1X 9DH

Phototypeset in Palatino and Celtic Hand using QuarkXPress on Apple Macintosh

Origination by Pixel Tech, Singapore
Printed by Hung Hing Offset Printing Co. Ltd., China

CONTENTS

INTRODUCTION 6

What are the Runes? 7   *Tracing Back the Runes* 9

The Futhark 8   *The Runes and the Tarot* 9

THE MAJOR ARCANA: THE RUNE CARDS 10

1. FEOH 12	9. HAEGL 28	17. TYR 44
2. UR 14	10. NYD 30	18. BIRCA 46
3. THORN 16	11. IS 32	19. EH 48
4. OS 18	12. GER 34	20. MAN 50
5. RAD 20	13. EOH 36	21. LAGU 52
6. KEN 22	14. PEORTH ... 38	22. ING 54
7. GYFU 24	15. EOLH 40	23. ODAL 56
8. WYN 26	16. SIGEL 42	24. DAEG 58

THE MINOR ARCANA: THE SEASONS 60

SPRING EQUINOX 64	AUTUMN EQUINOX 116
IMBOLC 66	LUGHNASADH 118
SUMMER SOLSTICE 90	WINTER SOLSTICE 142
BELTANE 92	SAMHAIN 144

THE LAYOUTS 168

THE CELTIC TREE LAYOUT 170
THE SEASONS LAYOUT 176
THE SUN WHEEL LAYOUT 179
FURTHER READING AND ACKNOWLEDGEMENTS 184

INTRODUCTION

*T*he Runic Tarot is a divination deck that uses the powerful symbolism of different, but closely interrelated, northern cultures. Over the centuries, Nordic and Celtic tribes fought, interacted, borrowed and influenced each other, taking what they found useful to enhance their own culture. The nature of divination is not an exclusive discipline. Tarot readers make use of astrology, astrologers may use a pendulum to verify difficult horary questions, and a psychic might use an eastern form of meditation to prepare for a clairvoyant consultation.

Each rune bears a meaning that signifies an important concept related to the everyday lives of the early peoples who used this divine wisdom. The need to predict and hopefully influence the outcome of their labours throughout the year demanded this magical link with the gods. Hence, every rune has a moral message to convey and a relationship to a Norse god. The meanings were largely based on the simple rhythmic lives of the farmers and tillers of the soil of earlier times. The seasons of planting, growth and fruition were the same for both the Celts and the Northern tribes, whose periods of celebration and worship were at similar times. To add time and accent to the powerful meanings of the runes, we have combined them with the four suits of the Celtic seasons that are inextricably linked with all life.

Just as each year has a spring, a summer, an autumn and a winter, so does each question asked of *The Runic Tarot*. With the runes set on the framework of the Sun's path around the zodiac, we can simply and clearly divine the answers to any of our current questions.

What are the Runes?

The runes are an ancient alphabet that the Germanic tribes used both for writing and divination. Ancient evidence of these strange markings reached as far as North America, probably through the early Viking seafarers who predated the voyage of Columbus by many centuries.

'Rune' means 'mystery' and 'secret' or 'secret council' and is found in most Germanic and Celtic languages, indicating the wide reach of runic lore among the Northern tribes of ancient Europe. Some authorities claim that the word was originally Celtic and borrowed from the Celtic tongue by Germanic peoples, though more have argued the reverse, since it is found with various different meanings in the Germanic family of languages.

There is much debate about the true origin of the runes, but in runic mythology we find the symbolic nature of these sigils truly expressed. The earth-linked symbolism of the secret markings is defined by the myth of the Norse god Odin, the tale of which is told in the poem *Havamal* (Song of the High One) from the *Elder Edda*, which is shown overleaf. The poet describes how Odin went through a self-imposed ordeal in order to gain something of great value for mankind. For nine days and nights he hung upside down from the world tree, Yggdrasil, with neither food nor drink, while being pierced by his own spear. During this ordeal he lost an eye, but the extraordinary shamanic experience revealed the runes as the great gift to all humanity that he was looking for. The runes brought forth the revelation of the secret forces of nature that made possible the development of true perception for ordinary mortals. The great gift of the transforming powers of the runes had been made available to all humankind.

This is a translation by W. H. Auden and P. B. Taylor, of part of the poem *Havamal*.

> *Wounded I hung on a wind-swept gallows*
> *For nine long nights,*
> *Pierced by a spear, pledged to Odhinn,*
> *Offered, myself to myself*
> *The wisest know not from whence spring*
> *The roots of that ancient rood.*
>
> *They gave me no bread,*
> *They gave me no mead,*
> *I looked down;*
> *With a loud cry*
> *I took up runes;*
> *From that tree I fell.*

The Futhark

The runes are divided into three sets of eight, called the aetts (families): Freya's Aett, Haegl's Aett and Tyr's Aett. The traditional name of these twenty-four runes is 'the Futhark', which is made up of the initial sound of the first few runes in the sequence: Feoh, Ur, Thorn, Os, Rad and Ken, in much the same way as our word 'alphabet' is based on the first two letters, 'a' and 'b', or the Greek, 'alpha' and 'beta'.

Tracing Back the Runes

Early runic inscriptions, including the whole set of runes in order, have been found on many objects such as swords, stones and bronze pendants. One of the most ancient is on the Kylver stone, discovered in Gotland, Sweden and dating from the fifth century CE. There are many others, though none as complete. The only written accounts of the runes are to be found in the many rune poems. There are verses that describe the meaning of each rune, and these can be found throughout the major arcana chapter of this book. The most famous piece is the old English rune poem by an anonymous poet, possibly a priest, the surviving manuscript dating back to around 1000 CE. It is thought that the writer may have lived many centuries before this and, even then, was writing of the mysterious markings that were ancient to him.

The Runes and the Tarot

In *The Runic Tarot* the twenty-four runes of the Elder Futhark form the most important part of the divination deck. As in the traditional tarot these are the major arcana and refer to quite personal matters affecting the querent (questioner). The four suits of the Celtic seasons give a framework of time and sequence in which the powerful imagery of the runes can be expressed. Both the runes and the Celtic seasons relate to the simple unfolding of our ancestors' lives through the predictable rhythm of each year, but apply with astonishing accuracy to the ups and downs of the present day. They focus on the natural progression of each event and idea that concerns our everyday lives, and can give meaning and guidance with regard to the final outcome.

THE MAJOR ARCANA

THE RUNE CARDS

As you become more familiar with the runes, you will discover that both the glyphs and the rune names exist in a number of different forms. This is understandable as communication from country to country and village to village was very limited during ancient times when the runes were becoming established. We have worked with the present variants of the rune shapes for many years, and the names that we use are, in the main, Old English.

As mentioned on page 8, the twenty-four runes are traditionally divided into three sections, or aetts. These are easily recognizable in the cards as they are numbered. Freya's Aett is 1 to 8, Haegl's Aett 9 to 16 and Tyr's Aett 17 to 24. The description of the aetts is mentioned frequently but is rarely explained. Perhaps the best interpretation of the three divisions is in the writing of D. Jason Cooper in his book *Esoteric Rune Magic*, where he ascribes them to an age-old division in Aryan tribal society – nurturer, warrior and priest or king. In medieval terms, this was translated as those who work, those who fight and those who pray. So, the first eight runes reflect nurturing, growing and sustaining life. The second eight are about the defence and protection of our rights and the last eight are concerned with our spiritual well-being. All are ruled by the element 'spirit', which gives rise to fire, earth, air and water (the four elements associated with the minor arcana).

The circular diagram opposite shows the twenty-four runes placed on the Sun's apparent path around the zodiac year. Around the outside are the three aetts displaying the zodiac signs and keywords attributed to each rune.

FREYA'S AETT

ᚠ	1	FEOH	ᛉ/ᛉ	Cattle, wealth
ᚾ	2	UR	ᛉ/ᛋ	Courage, a test
ᚦ	3	THORN	ᛋ/ᛋ	Attack or defence
ᚨ	4	OS	ᛋ/ᚋ	God, Odin, language
ᚱ	5	RAD	ᚋ/ᚋ	Journeys, in control
ᚲ	6	KEN	ᚋ/ᚊ	Fire, enlightenment
ᚷ	7	GYFU	ᚊ/ᚊ	Giving and taking, balance
ᚹ	8	WYN	ᚊ/ᚅ	Willing something into being, joy

HAEGL'S AETT

ᚺ	9	HAEGL	ᚅ/ᚅ	Destruction, transformation
ᚾ	10	NYD	ᚅ/ᛗ	Need, feeling the pinch
ᛁ	11	IS	ᛗ/ᛗ	Ice, frozen, stagnation
ᛄ	12	GER	ᛗ/≏	Harvest good or bad
ᛇ	13	EOH	≏/≏	Yew, endurance, death, change
ᛈ	14	PEORTH	≏/♏	Gamble, fate, fortune
ᛉ	15	EOLH	♏/♏	Protection, sedge grass
ᛋ	16	SIGEL	♏/♐	Sun, success, victory

MIDDAY
Culmination or Southing

JUN JUL AUG

SUNRISE IN THE EAST

BELTANE
SUMMER

IMBOLC
SPRING

S
E W
N

AUTUMN
LUGHNASADH

SUNSET IN THE WEST

WINTER
SAMHAIN

FEB JAN DEC

NIGHT

TYR'S AETT

ᛏ	17	TYR	♐/♐	Star, redressing the balance
ᛒ	18	BIRCA	♐/♑	Rebirth, awakening
ᛖ	19	EH	♑/♑	Trust, teamwork
ᛗ	20	MAN	♑/≈	Odin, Frigg, mankind
ᛚ	21	LAGU	≈/≈	Water, ebb and flow, intuition
ᛜ	22	ING	≈/♓	Life, seed, family
ᛟ	23	ODAL	♓/♓	Inheritance, ancestors
ᛞ	24	DAEG	♓/♈	Clarity, daylight

KEY TO ASTROLOGICAL SYMBOLS

♈	♉	♊	♋	♌	♍
ARIES	TAURUS	GEMINI	CANCER	LEO	VIRGO

♎	♏	♐	♑	♒	♓
LIBRA	SCORPIO	SAGITTARIUS	CAPRICORN	AQUARIUS	PISCES

1 FEOH 1

ϒ CATTLE, WEALTH ϒ

FEOH

CATTLE, WEALTH
ARIES
SPIRIT

VERSE I FEHU
Wealth is a consolation to all men
Yet much of it must each man give away
If glory he desire
To gain before his god.

This is the first rune of Freya's Aett and it is dedicated to the god of fertility, Freya. In the ancient world, wealth was measured by the ability to sustain a family, and cattle were of prime importance. People of wealth were expected to provide for those around them, hence Feoh denotes the use or misuse of power. Cattle as a symbol of wealth and prosperity implies two things. Firstly, the acquisition of great riches can be a good thing if shared with others, and secondly, there is an obligation to look after the riches with which to tend the cattle in order that they multiply and continue to sustain. Feoh represents plenty, but also insists that this wealth is shared with others to win favour and eventual fulfilment. Generosity is an important feature in Nordic culture.

Individuals or Events Represented by this Card

These include those who recognize the true value of things – that possessions are not an end in themselves but a means to an end – and people that realize that although money can give access to power, the most potent power is the potential within themselves.

This card can also signify over-dependence on a mother. When in company with spring cards, it may indicate brilliant insight into financial matters, but when winter cards are dominant it can show people who express an anger and forcefulness that may lead to frustration and loss of respect.

IN A READING

Achieved ambitions. Good health. Wealth.
Fulfilled love. Good fortune.
But all these come with a warning to be charitable and generous to others.
The symbolism of cattle in today's terms means movable wealth,
such as money and possessions.
Alternatively, Feoh can mean emotional and spiritual riches.

WHEN REVERSED

Failed plans and ambitions. Low vitality.
A financially lean time. Unrequited love.
A run of missed opportunities.

2 UR 2

COURAGE,
A TEST

♈ | COURAGE, A TEST | ♉

UR

COURAGE,
A TEST
ARIES/TAURUS
SPIRIT

VERSE II URUZ
The Aurochs is fearless and huge of horn
A ferocious beast, it fights with its horns
A famous moor-stalker that:
A mettlesome wight.

Ur is the second rune of the aett of Freya, and is the symbol for the wild ox or aurochs. Unlike the gentle cattle of the first rune, Feoh, that relate to prestige, possessions and sustenance, the aurochs is the primal raw force of nature that is both primitive and very strong. It symbolizes elemental masculine power and energy. Young warriors tested themselves on this now extinct animal, venturing out alone to hunt and hoping to bring back the horns to be used as prized drinking vessels. To tame this beast and bring it within one's domestic herd signified immense power and influence.

As Feoh represents the dynamic feminine potential for creation, Ur tells us that for the feminine to achieve this, it must develop and react with more masculine qualities including sheer brute strength, raw elemental power and determination.

Individuals or Events Represented by this Card

These include those who measure success in terms of the common good, and those who gather good fortune through the collective efforts of a group who share the fortunes equally. These people are an inspiration to us all, and have the ability to be shamans and healers. They excel at work that benefits others who understand the importance of an equal exchange of energy. They have a broad knowledge and are very physical and active. They make excellent social workers, lawyers, nurses, doctors and administrators. When they give advice, it is always worth listening.

IN A READING

Physical strength and speed, untamed potential.
A time of great energy and health. Sexual desire, masculine potency.
Freedom, energy, action, courage, strength, tenacity, understanding, wisdom.
Sudden or unexpected changes (usually for the better).
The shaping of power and pattern, formulation of the self.

WHEN REVERSED

Weakness, obsession, misdirected force, domination by others.
Sickness, inconsistency, ignorance.
Lust, brutality, rashness, callousness, violence.

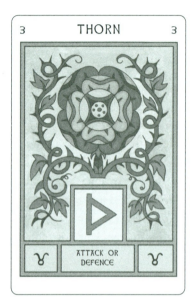

THORN

ATTACK OR DEFENCE
TAURUS
SPIRIT

VERSE III THURISAZ
The Thorn is sorely sharp for any thane
Hurtful to hold
Uncommonly severe
To every man who lies among them.

Thorn indicates that there will be difficulties or obstacles. These are not necessarily destructive, and often when we meet them they strengthen and teach us. All legendary heroes have dragons to slay or giants to fight! The message of this rune is 'to learn you must suffer'. This means not only physical suffering, but also allowing the inevitable to happen and experiencing all that life offers. As with the rose and the thorn, the gain can be worth the pain. What may at first appear to be a negative, destructive obstacle can later reveal itself to be a precious lesson, bringing about change and clearing the way for a new, creative beginning.

Individuals or Events Represented by this Card

People of power or position who pose a threat are represented here. Alternatively, this card can portray those who resist the temptation of great rewards if they can only be won through dishonesty or trickery. The energy of this rune can be used for good or for utter chaos. It represents the lower forces of the human psyche, and can indicate anger and lust. The thorn is dangerous if used as a weapon; it can pierce and wound. It can also provide secure protection, as with a thorny hedge. Occasionally, this rune signifies sudden good fortune but, more often, it is a warning that luck is running out.

IN A READING

*The Thorn card can indicate an important decision
and the power within to face anything.
A situation where power can corrupt if someone doesn't have
a true and honest heart.
It can show that the questioner is being too stubborn in the current situation,
to their detriment.*

WHEN REVERSED

*A great difficulty may be overcome.
A good omen. A sign that it is safe to go ahead.
The danger is passed.*

4	OS	4

GOD, ODIN, LANGUAGE

ᛟ · GOD, ODIN, LANGUAGE · ♊

OS

GOD,
ODIN,
LANGUAGE
TAURUS / GEMINI
SPIRIT

VERSE IV ANSUZ
The Mouth is the source of every speech,
The mainstay of wisdom,
And solace of sages,
And the happiness and hope of every eorl.

Os represents communication, creativity and controlled power. Traditionally, this is the rune of prophecy and revelation. It also encompasses the ideas of learning and reason, leading to teaching and the giving of good advice. In the magical sense, this rune refers to divine power and the invocation of assistance from the gods. Os provides both creative and spiritual inspiration. Language is vital here but in the broadest sense; this is the divine gift that enhances all manner of creative expression. Odin was not only the revealer of the runes; he was also the sorcerer of the gods. His magic is invariably more powerful than anyone else's. In a positive reading this rune will bring inspiration and brilliance. The message of Os is to explore our inner awareness and powers of self-expression, and to bring them in tune with the essence of the universe.

Individuals or Events Represented by this Card

Os can symbolize a role model or someone who can give good advice, such as a teacher or priest. It tells us that sometimes the answers to questions are available but not yet recognized. When this rune is dealt, we must look for signs and confirmations, which are all around: there is much of significance, and acceptance of this will lead to understanding. Ensure you don't ignore the message because you don't like the content. All experience is a lesson that teaches and, by accepting the truth, knowledge and wisdom will increase. Os may refer to a test or perhaps an interview. It can mean a letter, book or other form of information.

IN A READING

The querent will receive messages, or a gift of great worth.
The gift can also be a warning, telling that a situation must be avoided.
A message to explore your spiritual roots and study
the foundations of the universe.

WHEN REVERSED

A breakdown in communications and a need to consider other ways.
A caution to become more aware and careful.
Be wary of misinterpreting information.

RAD

JOURNEYS,
IN CONTROL
GEMINI
SPIRIT

VERSE V RAIDO
For every hero in the hall is Harness soft
And very hard for him who sits astride
A stout steed over miles of road.

Rad can simply mean ride or travel, although it also has a deeper meaning. The symbolism of riding a horse suggests both travel over distance and direction. A journey can be long and difficult, requiring planning, determination and fortitude. Rad can, therefore, refer to the querent's journey through life, and the search for a personal philosophy. It indicates the method required to achieve an aim or ambition but, also the road itself that must be taken. Rad, or Rit, has a secondary association with travel, which is the wheel. As well as the wheel that we all connect with travel, this can also be the wheel of the year, the Earth's movement around the Sun or the wheel of life. In more mundane terms, Rad can mean transport or communication, such as delivering or receiving messages or information, good advice or the application of common sense to everyday matters.

Individuals or Events Represented by this Card

These include people who are conscious of the rhythm and cycles of the year, and those who understand the necessity to proceed with determination through the difficult periods, in order to break through to easier times. Ideas inherent in this card are moral consciousness, freedom and great physical and mental movement. Rad represents those who are in charge of their lives and are open to changes of direction when and where the necessity arises. The essence of the Rad card is to be able to control and direct one's own journey through life.

IN A READING

A time when it is of supreme importance
to recognize the path you should take.
Rad can indicate a journey taken for pleasure or education.
Maybe this is a philosophical journey or an acquisition of new knowledge.
Work opportunities connected with transport or overseas locations.

WHEN REVERSED

Lack of movement or ability to change or move forward.
Isolation. A breakdown of plans.
A missed deadline or opportunity.

KEN

FIRE, ENLIGHTENMENT GEMINI / CANCER SPIRIT

VERSE VI KAUNO
A Torch alight is known to all alive
Brilliant and bright,
It burns most oft
Where aethlings rest themselves within.

The symbolic meanings of this card are light, enlightenment, warmth and fire. The rune symbol itself appears as the spread of a beam of light. It highlights the current situation and dispels the black shadows of ignorance. It encourages us to apply discernment to what we see and understand. Ken also reminds us of the healing warmth and companionship of the home fire and family well-being. It can represent a life transition moving from darkness and misunderstanding to clarity of purpose. There is a downside to Ken, which may manifest as revealing too much to the detriment of the situation. Fire brings light but it also brings heat, and it warns of the potential to burn our fingers if some moderation isn't shown.

Individuals or Events Represented by this Card

The Ken card represents those of great vision who can see the way ahead when others are uncertain, and individuals who look for ways in which to reveal truths to themselves and others. It can indicate a new study that will enrich the life of the one who embarks on it. Psychologically, it can represent close insight into the consciousness and an ability to sense the true meaning underlying any situation. Enlightenment itself is not the goal; it is the starting point of a life adventure that will give you great fulfilment in the ability to pass on to others the truth you have found.

IN A READING

Ken can indicate a revelation, a sudden inspiration.
It also indicates a time of great warmth and well-being.
A light shed on a new and exciting path.
Being in a position to receive or offer good advice.
Acting positively on newly acquired knowledge.

WHEN REVERSED

The clouding over of a situation that seemed at one time quite clear.
A message to let go of the restrictions of the past.

GYFU

GIVING AND TAKING, BALANCE
CANCER
SPIRIT

VERSE VII GEBO
Generosity in men is to honour and praise
And dignity a prop;
And for every wrack,
Riches and substance, who has naught else.

G yfu – rune number seven – is a gift, and is the origin of the belief that the number seven is lucky. It represents a gift in more than one sense – it can be a present, an attribute, or a certain skill or ability. In the past, a gift always required another in return. So, in accepting a gift you are placed under an obligation to the one who gives – the gods, fate or another person. Gyfu can also symbolize a relationship or team-work, in business or in love. The runic symbol of Gyfu is the one which we still use to represent the kiss, and when given or received it is, of course, the essence of mutual affection and love. However, it is neces-sary to find the balance between giving and receiving, and sense when it is appropriate.

Individuals or Events Represented by this Card

Gyfu represents the type of person who, on finding fame and fortune, desires to invest their riches in a charitable organization. 'Putting something back' is a fulfilling and necessary experience that enhances the pleasure of our own good fortune. Gyfu is also giving and receiving forgiveness – perhaps the greatest gift of all. It can indicate artistic and creative talent that must be practised, enjoyed and used for the pleasure of others. Above all, Gyfu is a symbol of the perfect balance of day-to-day giving and taking within a close, happy relationship or marriage.

IN A READING

Gyfu shows that if you ask forgiveness it will be given.

A gift, present or windfall is foretold.

Artistic or creative ability.

Sudden awareness of, or development of, an ability or talent.

To show compassion.

Being bold enough to declare your love.

Good fortune in a partnership matter.

WHEN REVERSED

This rune can't be reversed and therefore its meaning is constant.

WYN

WILLING SOMETHING INTO BEING, JOY
CANCER/LEO
SPIRIT

VERSE VIII WUNJO
He enjoys Delight who knows little of woe,
Of suffering and sorrow,
And has for his own prosperity, pleasure,
Eke the plenty of cities.

This rune is linked to earned rewards, a feeling of benevolence, and a life that runs smoothly because you have a positive and harmonious attitude. Wyn shows close co-operation and companionship with others, because joy is usually a shared emotion. It is easy to approach life's difficulties with negativity, yet it is important to allow the sheer joy of Wyn to reach into all areas of life, including the challenges. It tells us that happiness is promised if you are willing to work for it and strive for balance and harmony. Positive individuals have their foundations in complete truth and honesty. If we hide from the truth, then we hide from the opportunity of true happiness. Seek only your own truth, and happiness cannot fail to follow.

Individuals or Events Represented by this Card

The card of Wyn portrays people whose attitude to life is honest and positive, who set themselves a target and allow nothing to stand in their way. It represents those who, with great determination, seek to achieve a better life for those who are less fortunate. Wyn can simply express a period of great joy in our lives. This rune is said to be associated with the Nordic god Odin as the fulfiller of wishes. It is about setting our heart on something and believing in the good fortune for it to become a reality.

IN A READING

The realization of a longed-for ambition.

Success in finding romance.

A period of good health and vitality.

Partnerships that develop positively.

New ventures are fortunate.

A successful period for creative work.

Something that has suddenly been perfected or improved beyond expectations.

WHEN REVERSED

Misunderstanding. Romance or partnership problems.

Ambitions blocked in some way. A difficult time for new ventures.

9   HÆGL   9

HÆGL

DESTRUCTION, TRANSFORMATION
LEO
SPIRIT

VERSE IX HAGALAZ
Hail is the whitest of grain
Whirled from heaven's height,
The wind hurls it in showers
Into water then it turns.

Haegl, the ninth rune and first rune of Haegl's Aett, has the basic meaning hail, and its portent may be likened to a sudden unexpected hailstorm, an unfortunate disruption of one's way of life. It can suggest limitation, interruption or delay, and imply an unwanted or forced change in direction. Haegl can symbolize suffering, hardship, illness or injury. The imagery of the weather in Haegl's verse can also be taken literally and it would be wise to insure against storm damage, floods or lightning. There is always an indication of disruptive influences at work when this rune appears. Positively, it can show that challenges are occurring in your life. These are not to be feared, but bravely faced. A violent hailstorm is unpleasant and painful, but if you examine a hailstone you will see that it is only water that easily melts in your hand. So, when facing a trial, the heat of your determination can melt all opposition.

Individuals or Events Represented by this Card

These include people who seem to have lost everything and yet are prepared to buckle down and make an enthusiastic fresh start. It shows a period when our achievements go unrecognized, as if others are too distracted or blinded to our worth. It is often the 'spanner in the works' that disrupts everything and makes us sit up from our complacency. At these times, if we are forced to make choices, we begin to realize what the most important things are to us. Haegl is the inevitable – the harsh reminder that nothing is certain.

IN A READING

Disruption of the status quo.
A sudden challenge, which if met bravely can enhance the quality of life.
A discovery that the time has come for breaking destructive patterns and removing unwanted influences.

WHEN REVERSED

Haegl has no reverse. Its meanings are the same however the card falls.

10   NYD   10

ℌ   NEED, FEELING THE PINCH   ♍

NYD

NEED,
FEELING THE PINCH
LEO / VIRGO
SPIRIT

VERSE X NAUDIZ
Hardship lies heavy on the heart
Yet oft to the children of men
It becomes nonetheless a help and a healing,
If they heed it in time.

Nyd represents need, hardship and adversity. Luckily, it also gives us the endurance to persevere, and backs up our reserves of inner strength. We must be assured though that however unpleasant the hardship, it will be a learning experience that will ultimately benefit us. Nyd can also be a warning against taking the easy but self-destructive path, so this card often appears to be the very opposite of what is wanted. But this situation won't last, and will be a lesson in making the transition from negative to positive. Our past may have conditioned us into thinking that we have needs that are actually no longer relevant and, by deprivation, Nyd shows us that maybe these are better left behind. It is necessary to understand and accept our past, but also to keep our minds fixed on the present – the only place where we have influence.

Individuals or Events Represented by this Card

Nyd represents people who seem to be continually struggling against the wind and overwhelming odds. These include the poor and those who bravely carry on making the best of an unenviable situation, and also those who live frugally and simply in order to reach a more spiritual and less materialistic way of life. This card can show a creative block or an inability to come up with answers in a demanding situation. One's thinking can be limited and dulled by lack of inspiration. Nyd can herald a period of delays and frustrations that will need unlimited patience.

IN A READING

It isn't good to fight against an adverse situation – use it to your advantage.
Using an upset to better yourself.
Disciplining yourself by getting rid of bad or self-indulgent habits.

WHEN REVERSED

There are hidden drawbacks contained within your desires.
A seemingly lavish acquisition has strings attached.

11   IS   11

mp | ICE, FROZEN, STAGNATION | mp

IS

ICE,
FROZEN,
STAGNATION
VIRGO
SPIRIT

VERSE XI ISA
Ice is extremely cold, immeasurably slippery.
It glistens clear as glass;
Most like to gems.
Is a floor wrought of frost a fair sight?

The meaning of Is is ice. Although the sudden appearance of ice on a winter's day can be beautiful, it can also be treacherous. It can be slippery or dangerously thin, or make progress impossible. Is means that you may have to delay your ambitions until a more favourable season. Positively though, Is can cool down a heated confrontation, or protect against magical attack. Emotionally, it suggests a cooling of affection, or frigidity. It has a freezing, delaying or preserving effect on other runes that appear in the same reading. It indicates a period of non-action. It is a time when we may realize that we are in a rut, unable to escape and move on to a more exciting existence. Things appear to be at a standstill but this is not a time to try to force change: great patience and wisdom are called for. It is an opportunity to rest, rethink and reaffirm ambitions.

Individuals or Events Represented by this Card

These include people who have settled into a set way of life that involves little change, and those who obstinately resist change, even to their own detriment. This card is a powerful tool for those who use this time positively for slowing down, recuperating and waiting for a more refreshed situation. It can mean a frustrating time if we are forced to wait. Just as spring's young shoots can be damaged by the frost, a reality that arises too soon is affected negatively by the appearance of Is. The seedlings must hold back until warmer weather takes over.

IN A READING

Make positive use of an unavoidable hold-up.
Stop efforts that are showing no results.
Coolness in those around you hides unspoken emotions.
A possible change will turn out to be of no benefit.
Smiles mask adverse intentions.

WHEN REVERSED

Is has no reverse but has both positive and negative meanings.

GER

HARVEST
GOOD OR BAD
VIRGO / LIBRA
SPIRIT

VERSE XII JERA
Harvest is the hope of men, then the gods,
Heaven's holy Kings,
Allows the earth to yield
To prince and pauper, glorious fruits.

Ger, as rune number twelve, represents the months of the year and the signs of the zodiac. It implies fruitfulness, profit or achievement of our aims. It also means the cycle of the seasons, suggesting change and natural, predictable development. It is mostly a positive rune, but will always result in the natural outcome of past actions. Ger can, for this reason, represent justice, which may be positive or negative – reward or punishment. This is a time to benefit from the hard work we have carried out in the past, a time of flourishing harvest, of joy and satisfaction. It is, however, after a brief celebration, essential to continue work without complacency. The yearly harvest is followed closely by winter, so ensure you have enough stored reserves to face the next stage of the cycle.

Individuals or Events Represented by this Card

People who work on the land or with their hands receive great rewards. Ger represents successes and the fruition of long-term plans. It can indicate a turning in life, an offer of work requiring perseverance and endurance with outstanding results. This card includes those who are at one with the seasons and who live a gentle and hopeful life, and it represents the successful completion of a cycle. The harvest you gain at this time is stored for the lean times ahead. Great support and respect are gained by the sharing of your good fortune.

IN A READING

Patience is rewarded.

A time of abundance not to be taken for granted.

Developing as yet undiscovered talents.

Sharing your talents with others.

A celebration or holiday taken before a time of renewed hard work.

WHEN REVERSED

Ger has no reverse.

| 13 | EOH | 13 |

YEW, ENDURANCE, DEATH, CHANGE

EOH

YEW, ENDURANCE, DEATH, CHANGE

LIBRA

SPIRIT

VERSE XIII IHWAZ
The Yew is a rough tree without,
Fixed hard in the earth, the fire's herd,
Sustained by its roots,
A delight on the homeland.

Eoh is the symbol of runic magic. It enables us to avert or deflect danger and enhances our defensive power, and reveals patience, foresight and protection against unexpected dangers from others. It is symbolized by the yew tree and is mistakenly linked with death because of the popular planting of these trees in graveyards. This has also led to the superstitious belief that the number thirteen is unlucky. The real reason for planting these great trees was to keep out scavenging beasts – the evergreen yew is a protection for any property in that it is both poisonous and impenetrable. Eoh should not be seen as negative, as it also means continuation and endurance. The famous English long-bows were traditionally made from yew trees and, as well as being powerful, long-lasting, and extremely flexible, they contained great protective magic. It follows that Eoh indicates safety from attack and a magical weapon for our defence.

Individuals or Events Represented by this Card

People who are able to accept change and transformation are portrayed by the card of Eoh. It represents a time for letting go of the old and embracing the new, and gives us the courage to take a step into the dark, knowing that we are protected from danger. If referring to a new venture, this card will show that with the accumulation of experience and life knowledge, now is the time to take the risk. Eoh teaches that the only constant is change, and positive progress requires the acceptance of change and not resistance to it.

IN A READING

At a difficult time you are secure from danger.
Making a stand and defending a point of view.
Protecting a loved one.
The courage to act swiftly and move forward.

WHEN REVERSED

Eoh has no reverse.

PEORTH

GAMBLE,
FATE,
FORTUNE

LIBRA / SCORPIO

SPIRIT

VERSE XIV PERTH
The Peorth is ever the play and laughter
Of proud men …
Where warriors sit blithely
Together in the beer-hall.

P eorth means a gamble or a mystery. Its symbol is said to represent the dice cup and warns of a chance being taken that could have an uncertain outcome. The way the dice fall reflects our lot in life and we can only do our best with what we are presented with. Because of its association with gambling and chance, Peorth has come to portend secrets, both hidden and revealed. Indeed, its nature is always concerned with something secret. The other runes in the reading will help to show the nature of the secret. Maybe because there is a womblike imagery to the dice cup and the aura of fate that permeates this card, it is often the herald of a birth. The processes of birth are mysterious and hidden, later to be revealed in the arrival of the baby.

Individuals or Events Represented by this Card

This card can describe someone who has something to hide – a cheater or confidence trickster. Conversely, it can represent someone who reveals a secret to you. Because of the mystery surrounding it, common sense and some reservations are called for in the way you interpret Peorth. It has an uncanny way of reversing any outcome that you may predict for its particular position in the reading. As with the Wheel of Fortune in the traditional tarot, Peorth is the symbol of fate and its very essence is the unexpected.

IN A READING
Something hidden is revealed.
Conversely, something hidden may remain so.
A new facet of yourself may be discovered.
A rebirth.
Something unplanned that completely changes your life direction.

WHEN REVERSED
Be wary of risk taking.
An emotional impasse.
Something hidden should be left well alone.

EOLH

PROTECTION,
SEDGE GRASS
SCORPIO
SPIRIT

VERSE XV ALGIZ
The Elk's-sedge has its home most oft in the fen.
It waxes in water, wounds grimly.
The blood burns of every man
Who makes any grasp at it.

Eolh symbolizes the antlers of the elk and the shape of the herb sedge grass. Suggesting the outspread fingers of a hand raised in defence, it's the most powerful rune of protection, and on a spiritual plane it denotes reaching up to the gods. Eolh also represents achievement in a venture or quest, through extreme tenacity and endeavour. Just as the sedge has sharp, swordlike leaves, we will be protected from outside harm. Like the sedge we will be sharp, alert and aware of every extreme possibility of our venture. Wisdom and acute vision will assist the cause. The sedge that so well protects is a danger if not handled properly. In foolish hands it can become a self-inflicting weapon. It will serve its guardian well if handled with the greatest value and respect.

Individuals or Events Represented by this Card

Eolh can describe someone who has great confidence borne out of honourable service. It represents those who are careful how they use any power they have and how they treat those around them. When this rune appears, it is telling you that although the path ahead is filled with danger, you can be fearless, for you have the power of protection within you. You will be secure for as long as you are not complacent. Eolh indicates that the time is ripe for undertaking risky ventures, although even now it would be wise to ensure you have reasonably firm foundations.

IN A READING

A protective influence that can counter more difficult runes.

A contact with higher powers.

A challenge to be taken bravely.

WHEN REVERSED

Self-inflicted problems.

Being taken advantage of.

A warning against making a decision.

Not taking risks.

SIGEL

SUN, SUCCESS, VICTORY

SCORPIO / SAGITTARIUS

SPIRIT

VERSE XVI SOWILO
The Sun is ever the hope of seamen
When they fare over the fishes' bath,
Until the sea-steed
Brings them to land.

S igel glows with the energy of the Sun. It is the spirit of life, complete spiritual awareness and unlimited energy. It is a rune of good health and is warming to the spirit. Just as the Sun lights up the world, so the symbolism of this rune illuminates the life of those it touches. Perception becomes clear and the gift of understanding is made available. It is the spirit of life and the energy of the Sun. It is completeness, spiritual awareness, boundless energy and strength of character. It also indicates a capacity to learn. Although Sigel is traditionally known as a victory symbol, it can also be used as a positive and enlightening force of creativity. It symbolizes the natural power of the Sun, clear vision, and the victory of light over darkness, good over evil.

Individuals or Events Represented by this Card

This card can describe people of clear vision and creative visualization, those who fight adversity, be it injustice, poverty or crime. The light of the Sun is powerful and nothing can hide from its brilliance. That which has been hidden is brought to light. Psychologically, Sigel can indicate a self-revelation or a deeper consciousness of the inner-self. Extra power is gained in order to bring things to fruition. Good fortune awaits and there is a positive feel to everything. This is no time to look far ahead for solutions to current problems; the answers are within your grasp.

IN A READING

An abundance of energy to apply to a current situation.
Becoming conscious of your true path.
Spiritual guidance.

WHEN REVERSED

Sigel has no reverse.

17   TYR   17

STAR, REDRESSING
THE BALANCE

TYR

STAR,
REDRESSING THE BALANCE
SAGITTARIUS
SPIRIT

VERSE XVII TIWAZ
Tiw is a certain sign; it keeps trust well
With aethlings; ever on course
Over the night-fogs,
It never falls.

Tyr, the first rune of Tyr's Aett, is named after the Norse god Tiw, who is still remembered by us in the day of Tiw, Tuesday. He was the equivalent of the great gods Jupiter and Zeus. The image represents the spear of the god Tiw, who was the god of war, justice, law and order, and success through self-sacrifice. He allowed the Ferris Wolf to bite off his right hand in order to bind the wolf's chaotic force and thus is known as the protector of warriors, the disabled and the left-handed. Tyr denotes courage, bravery, dedication and daring. Because of its protective qualities, amulets of this rune were made to keep those who wore them safe from harm on sea voyages. This powerful rune signifies determination and male sexuality, new challenges and the revelation of new understanding. It shows leadership potential and self-belief in adverse situations.

Individuals or Events Represented by this Card

Tyr can describe those going into a battle of some kind or taking up a challenge. It shows situations where there is a need for real courage, although victory will be assured if your heart remains honest and true. It is a call to utilize all the skill and wisdom you have acquired through life to cope with this supreme moment. This card can show a need to protect beliefs that will certainly be challenged and put to the test. Like the spear image, it shows you are on a clear, straight path to victory.

IN A READING

A feeling of extra power and support.
A competition or challenge that you feel well able to enter.
The backing of someone in a position of authority or influence.

WHEN REVERSED

Battling against great odds.
Danger of losing a contest or law suit.
A tendency to cowardice.
Chickening out.
Loss of concentration.

BIRCA

REBIRTH, AWAKENING
SAGITTARIUS / CAPRICORN
SPIRIT

VERSE XVIII BERKANAN
The Birch is fruitless, nonetheless it bears
Shoots without seed; it is beauteous in boughs
High of helm, fairly adorned
Laden with leaves, close to the sky.

This rune signifies the birch tree, which symbolizes fertility. There are many instances in European folk tradition where the beating of birch twigs is used to encourage prosperity and guarantee conception. There's an English tradition that survives in some communities, where the young men are sent out to 'beat the bounds of the parish' with branches of birch to ensure prosperity in the countryside in the coming year. As Tyr is the fundamental male archetype, Birca is the equivalent for women, for it represents the role of the mother, the healer and the midwife, bringing forth new life following death just as the birch tree produces the first leaves after a hard winter. The imagery of birth can be both literal and symbolic, so is just as likely to refer to the start of a new venture as to the birth of a baby.

Individuals or Events Represented by this Card

Those described by Birca are concerned with their own regeneration, purification and recovery. It represents those making a major life change in terms of health and philosophy. It is the rune of the make-over and the transformation, the family and the home, and symbolizes the pleasure of sexual relations. It heralds a period of physical or mental growth, increased business both in investment and profit, and a year of bumper crops. It indicates lost causes that may be reclaimed and new beginnings that will flourish.

IN A READING

An exciting time for fresh beginnings and new adventures.
Spiritual renewal.
The acceptance of new ideas.
A decision to change your life.

WHEN REVERSED

Lack of development or reduction in status.
Decline or loss of business and profits.
A difficult time for new ventures.

19   ЄH   19

M

TRUST,
TEAMWORK

ЄH

TRUST,
TEAMWORK
CAPRICORN
SPIRIT

VERSE XIX EHWAZ
A Steed is the joy of aethlings or eorls,
A horse proud of hoof, where men about it,
Wealthy, on stallions, swap speech,
And to the unquiet is ever a solace.

The traditional meaning of this rune is the horse, dealing with movement, travel and, more specifically, the vehicle of that travel. For this reason, most students of the runes see this image as a pair of horses. It indicates great power and control, as would be necessary if driving a chariot and a pair of steeds. It is related to a big change of location and the need to travel great distances in order to achieve our desire. It also describes close teamwork and partnership, where each individual involved is totally reliant on everybody else for the continuous smooth running of the journey. The horse is a powerful servant but must be carefully controlled to avoid harming itself or others. It is exhilarating to just go galloping along thoughtlessly, but to do so is to risk losing that special power permanently. A balance must be achieved.

Individuals or Events Represented by this Card
These include those who are confident and proud of their achievements, but remain in control in order to reach a safe conclusion to their journey. Eh also represents those who are team leaders with a group of highly individualistic, but creatively talented, members. It is good to remember that the horse is a source of motion and energy but it is also a living, breathing creature with needs and desires that must be taken into consideration, rather than simply being used as a slave. With this rune there comes a responsibility for the well-being of the source of power.

IN A READING
Embarking on a journey or major new experience.
Taking on a greater position of responsibility.
The pleasure of getting on with new people or a new team.
Joining a team. A change of country or home.
Support from others in your current projects.

WHEN REVERSED
End of a partnership. A loss.
An opportunity missed through overenthusiasm.
Going too far. Riding roughshod over others.

20   MAN   20

ODIN, FRIGG, MANKIND

MAN

ODIN, FRIGG, MANKIND

CAPRICORN/AQUARIUS

SPIRIT

VERSE XX MANNAZ
A mirthful Man is to his kinsmen dear;
Yet each one must from the others turn,
Because Odin desires by his decree
To deliver that frail flesh to earth.

The traditional meaning of Man is all of mankind. In another sense though, it is the self. It is being at one with yourself, knowing yourself and the point from which all other relationships flow. It is yourself, your mind and ego, your body. It is the concept that we are all one family together, and yet each of us is alone in our final journey. It is our contact with the gods and is particularly associated with the Nordic gods Odin and Frigg. This card portrays the entire network of human relationships with the self at the centre, and reflects the reality of our lives. Our interdependence as human beings is paramount, and to feel supported and to be able to give support in return is implied in the nature of this rune. Man indicates creativity, intelligence, forward planning and discussion, and counsels co-operation between individuals for the common good.

Individuals or Events Represented by this Card

This rune represents people of power who understand the needs of others, such as diplomats who seek to bring disputing countries to the discussion table. Also included here are those prepared to devote their lives to their fellow humans in whatever way they can. Man represents networking and keeping contacts and information on a large scale. For good or bad, the internet is humanity's greatest present-day tool for sharing its hopes and fears for this planet. Man is a symbol of our home and represents all those who our lives touch during our short stay on Earth.

IN A READING

Help given in solving a problem. Good advice.
Being carried along on the success of a group. Sharing good fortune.
Becoming part of a club or organization of those with shared interests.
An important discussion from which you gain a great deal.

WHEN REVERSED

Being left 'holding the baby'. A refusal or rejection.
Needing assistance or someone to tell your troubles to.
A feeling of alienation from those around you.
Taking the unpopular decision.

21 LAGU 21

WATER, EBB AND
FLOW, INTUITION

LAGU

WATER,
EBB AND FLOW,
INTUITION
AQUARIUS
SPIRIT

VERSE XXI LAGUZ
Water seems interminable to men
If they should venture on a shaky bark;
And the sea-surges greatly frighten them,
And the sea-steed takes no heed of the curb.

Lagu has associations with water in all its forms. It represents the cleansing action of the ocean's great tides – the ebb and flow. It is a vital part of life which we need to survive, and yet we can drown in its merciless power. Because of its fluctuating nature, water is the symbol of emotions and feelings. As a fortuitous omen for overseas travel, fishing and other aquatic activities, Lagu contains elements of fluidity, changeability and often, lack of control. Most people consider the symbolic meaning of water to be gentleness, sensitivity, love and intuition. For the Norse warriors the sea was a fearsome and unpredictable place, calling on all their staunch courage and seamanship to avoid it becoming a watery grave. The power of water is enormous, wearing down the hardest stone. In much the same way, our emotions are resilient and capable of surviving the most difficult of experiences.

Individuals or Events Represented by this Card

Lagu represents those who are prepared to take on the task of helping others through a self-examination process. It allows counsellors to empathize more strongly and share their own experiences. It describes the unconscious, intuitive and psychic abilities we may have. It can be deceptive, but this comes from its fluctuation more than from any true menace. Traditionally, it can be said that Lagu is another feminine rune in its caring and empathetic nature.

IN A READING

A feeling of being emotionally balanced and in harmony with life around you.
A fulfilling period, caring for others. Being cared for yourself.
The thrill of a new relationship or love affair.
A clairvoyant insight or vision.
Development of psychic abilities.

WHEN REVERSED

Emotional upset because of a misunderstanding.
A situation where you are being misled. A regretted temptation.
Warning of a dangerous emotional situation.

22	ING	22

LIFE, SEED, FAMILY

ING

LIFE, SEED, FAMILY AQUARIUS / PISCES SPIRIT

VERSE XXII INGWAZ
Ing was among the East-Danes first seen by men,
'Til later east he went over the wave;
His wain followed after;
The Headings named the hero so.

This rune is named after the Norse hero-god Ing, who came from across the sea to unite his restless people of Viking Jutland, and returned having established a country of peace and harmony. The image of this rune can be interpreted as a field, reminding us of the importance of our closeness to the earth and the feeling of being at one with nature. No matter how far from this we have strayed, Ing grounds us and reconnects our body, mind and spirit with our basic roots. But its real significance lies in its balance, representing the harmonious relationship between ourselves and the four elements or four directions. It's a reminder of the ancient belief in contact between the gods and the Earth, and unites us with our spiritual nature through close contact with the physical world.

Individuals or Events Represented by this Card

Ing describes those people who are close to nature or at one with their surroundings, and those who are concerned with the fertilization of the earth in anticipation of next year's crops. It represents the preparation or groundwork necessary to bring about the success of a project or idea, and can show the end of one cycle and the beginning of the next. It also indicates the generation and regeneration of life within the family. Ing honours a time of joyful celebration of new life and new growth.

IN A READING

Fertility.

A birth.

The preparation for the start of a new project.

Going 'back to basics'.

A period of calm after a storm.

Giving up the old way of doing things and making a fresh start.

A new job or occupation.

WHEN REVERSED

Ing has no reverse.

ODAL

INHERITANCE, ANCESTORS
PISCES
SPIRIT

VERSE XXIII OTHILA
An Estate is greatly dear to every man
If what is right and fitting there
He may enjoy at home
With most prosperity.

Odal means the land of our birth, our home, property and fixed wealth or inheritance. This can include the characteristics that you have inherited from your ancestors and will pass down to your children; Odal can also represent the strength of a united family and unique historical background. It is the sum total of all that you have accumulated and inherited during your time on Earth: possessions, beliefs, talents and family wisdom. The idea of inheritance or property is only a symbol – it shows that we must each search for our own 'centre' to add to our life's true meaning, and this is ultimately the goal of the runic journey. We will need to travel far away from our origins, either mentally or physically, in order to see clearly who and what we are. When we are sure, then and then alone, can we safely make the journey back home.

Individuals or Events Represented by this Card

Odal can represent ancestors who have been a strong influence in our life. It can describe our identification with family themes, such as medical, musical or farming occupations that continue through generations. It can show those who are interested in family history or genealogy. It may also describe the legal side of an inheritance and the passing on of legacies. Often Odal indicates giving something up in order to acquire a family possession or attribute. This may be an inevitable legacy and a responsibility where the individual has little choice in the matter.

IN A READING
Being left something in a will. Taking up a family occupation.
The acquiring of a family possession. Going back to your roots.
Starting from the beginning.

WHEN REVERSED
A disappointment in the family.
An inheritance that turns out to be worthless.
Feeling cut off from the family.
A family loss.

24   DÆG   24

CLARITY,
DAYLIGHT

DÆG

CLARITY,
DAYLIGHT
PISCES / ARIES
SPIRIT

VERSE XXIV DAGAZ
Day is Odin's messenger, dear to men,
The Ruler's glorious light,
Mirth and hope to prosperous and poor,
Useful to all.

The twenty-fourth and final rune, Daeg means day. Up in the Northern lands of long long nights and winters, the welcome daylight is strongly associated with vitality and re-energizing power. Daeg is the essence of natural light, the fresh crisp light of dawn, and the healing power of the Sun. Spiritually, it is the god-given illumination, the high point of the eternal cycle of dark–light–dark. Daeg symbolizes brilliance, growth, progress and development and often indicates a positive change. It is a breakthrough, like a ray of sun through the clouds. It is a sudden change of fortune to a period of success and prosperity, a new dawn or a major change of direction. It suggests achievement and a successful conclusion to a creative period. The blackness of night is left behind and a new day has begun. The warmth and light shines on rich and poor alike.

Individuals or Events Represented by this Card

Daeg can indicate those people who clearly reveal great truths and new knowledge, and those who bring hidden or unjust things to the light, causing a drastic change of public opinion. It can refer to individuals who research and discover new advances in the understanding of ourselves and our universe. It can mean a new way of living or a different way of seeing life. It is a period of divine protection, bringing with it the assurance that we are being assisted in the journey to our goal.

IN A READING

A flash of inspiration.

An extreme change in your way of life.

A sudden switch of fortunes to the benefit of the querent.

A sign of great strength with which to face the way ahead.

A renewal.

WHEN REVERSED

Daeg has no reverse.

THE MINOR ARCANA

THE SEASONS

The seasons are an integral part of our lives. Each event has a spring, a summer, an autumn and a winter; a start, a flowering, a harvest and a rest to renew life. As shown clearly in the twelve signs of the zodiac, the season of the year in which you were born influences your approach to life. The winter born are more comfortable with matters involving maintenance and survival than the happy-go-lucky summer born. Those who are born in the spring have a natural strength of will and courage with which to state their place in the world. The autumn born use the fruits of their talents for shared well-being. This rhythm is in every act, event and situation that we encounter, and as long as we understand at what stage or in which season it is placed, we can predict the next phase and the most likely outcome. For instance, if we are approaching winter we can't expect fruition and harvest, but must prepare for rest and rejuvenation. This simple law of nature is deep within all of us, and is part of our inheritance that can be seen in the yearly celebrations that we share with our earth-aware ancestors. The seasons, the Sun and Moon cycles and the appearance of the stars and planets are all part of our intuitive inheritance. We do not have to learn them, only remember them.

The table opposite shows the organization of the minor arcana cards by season, month and week through the Celtic year.

△ FIRE

🌱
IMBOLC
SPRING QUARTER

F E B	1 2 3 4	♒/♈ ♒/♉ ♒/♊ ♓/♋	PLANS
M A R	5 6 7 8	♓/♌ ♓/♍ ♓/♎ ♈/♏	CHALLENGE 21 MARCH SPRING EQUINOX
A P R	9 10 11 12	♈/♐ ♈/♑ ♈/♒ ♉/♓	PERSEVERANCE

▽ WATER

❀
BELTANE
SUMMER QUARTER

M A Y	1 2 3 4	♉/♈ ♉/♉ ♉/♊ ♊/♋	CONFIDENCE
J U N	5 6 7 8	♊/♌ ♊/♍ ♊/♎ ♋/♏	LOVE 21 JUNE SUMMER SOLSTICE
J U L	9 10 11 12	♋/♐ ♋/♑ ♋/♒ ♌/♓	FEASTING

⊿ EARTH

🍃
LUGHNASADH
AUTUMN QUARTER

A U G	1 2 3 4	♌/♈ ♌/♉ ♌/♊ ♍/♋	MATURITY
S E P	5 6 7 8	♍/♌ ♍/♍ ♍/♎ ♎/♏	HARVEST 23 SEPTEMBER AUTUMN EQUINOX
O C T	9 10 11 12	♎/♐ ♎/♑ ♎/♒ ♏/♓	RESOURCEFULNESS

▽ AIR

❄
SAMHAIN
WINTER QUARTER

N O V	1 2 3 4	♏/♈ ♏/♉ ♏/♊ ♐/♋	PREPARATION
D E C	5 6 7 8	♐/♌ ♐/♍ ♐/♎ ♑/♏	REST 22 DECEMBER WINTER SOLSTICE
J A N	9 10 11 12	♑/♐ ♑/♑ ♑/♒ ♒/♓	RENEWAL

The Four Suits

Each of the four seasons starts on, and is named for, its significant festival day.

SEASON	FESTIVAL	PRONUNCIATION	DATE
Spring	*Imbolc*	*Imm'ulk*	*1 February*
Summer	*Beltane*	*Bell'tane*	*1 May*
Autumn	*Lughnasadh*	*Loo'nassa*	*1 August*
Winter	*Samhain*	*Sow'en*	*1 November*

The minor arcana cards are divided into the four suits of the seasons, representing the rhythm of the Sun's path through a year. While the major arcana is formed of the traditional runes and the card illustrations reflect the widespread meanings that are associated with them, the minor arcana are a new invention and therefore require a more explanatory approach. For this reason, the interpretations of the minor cards each include a short description of the card image to assist users in identifying with, and getting to know, the cards.

The Four Trump Cards

The two Equinox and two Solstice cards in the Runic Tarot are the key astrological moments of the Sun's cycle as it moves into each of the four cardinal zodiac signs: Aries, Cancer, Libra and Capricorn. The image on each of the cards is the seasonally changing 'Green Man' – the god that dies and is reborn each year. This is the deeply hidden image of the movement of the seasons that manifested at different times as the Green Man, The Old Man of the Woods, Jack in the Green and even Robin Hood. There is a Gallic Green Man in local folklore in the verdant and earthy Charente in the South West of France, where I am writing this book and where Caroline has produced her beautiful paintings. The face surrounded in leaves is, in one form or another, seen in carvings in churches and old stonework across Europe, and is so strong in our earliest folklore that he was even accepted into Christian churches for fear of losing the support of the local communities.

SPRING EQUINOX

Sun in Aries on or around 21 March

The Spring (or Vernal) Equinox celebrates the crossover point between the dark and the light halves of the year. At this time the day and the night are of equal length. This is the time when the Sun enters Aries, the first Fire sign, underlining a new beginning. In ancient times, at this time of year, offerings were made to the shrine of Eostre, the fertility goddess of the Anglo Saxons. It is thought that her name comes from the word 'east', the direction of the rising Sun. Eggs were painted and offered as symbols of the fertility they hoped the goddess would bless them with. When life was more nature based, hens started producing eggs again at the time of the Spring Equinox, after their long resting period of winter. Eostre's sacred animal was the hare, and this old pagan festival lives on today in the form of the Easter Bunny and chocolate eggs. Eostre was also offered simple cakes that may have been similar to the hot cross buns that are now made and sold at this time. As with most of the early festivals, bonfires were lit to herald the rebirth of energy and light. Old corn dollies would be burned and their ashes scattered over the prepared earth of the fields. As a symbol of new life and renewal, we continue the ancient concept of spring-cleaning – throwing away the old and worthless clutter of the previous year to make way for the new. Although some of our ancestors may have had little time for the extremes of house-proudness, this was a special ceremony related to the concept of dark to light, new for old. It was powerful magic and still we act it out, not quite knowing why.

IN A READING

It is important to look at the general implication of the other cards close by. They will be enhanced or influenced by this powerful card and it will always indicate that despite other conditions, a new beginning, opportunity or a second chance will be of great significance to the successful outcome of the question.

IMBOLC
CARD 1

Season SPRING
Keyword SPONTANEITY
Element FIRE
Month FEBRUARY
Week 1ST
Astrology AQUARIUS / ARIES

THE IMAGE: *A horse breathing fire carries a rider with long hair flowing wildly. Both rider and animal are highly decorated and confidently bold. Below is water and an arc of the Sun's path through the stars. There is a sense of immediacy and boldness.*

The number one card of the spring suit combines the nature of the first sign, Aries, with the meaning of the Sun's early February position in Aquarius. The keyword produced by this combination is 'spontaneity' – quick action in response to an event based purely on a gut feeling. Aquarius is always ready to try out the new and innovative, and Aries must have immediate action at all costs. This is the trigger for the start of the growing year, the bursting out of the first brave shoots through the hard winter earth. This is a small but brave beginning. Delicate but determined, the heroic seedlings respond to a pulse from the earth, and are in tune with it as it spins around the Sun. The start of a brand new cycle is under way. The revolutionary nature of Aquarius accepts nothing at face value, and will spontaneously act in a contrary manner to provoke a reaction from which they may learn something new. When Aries has a job to be done, it gets done – immediately!

IN A READING

Quick action taken on your own with no recourse to help or advice.
An impulsive response to a difficult situation.
An on-the-spot decision that turns out well.
Quick action that becomes necessary in order not to miss an opportunity.
A decision made that contains an element of risk.
Throwing yourself into the limelight.

WHEN REVERSED

Losing something of value through being overcautious.
Worrying about what other people will think.
Being frightened of taking a step into the unknown.
Feeling apprehensive about a decision that has to be made.
Feeling restless and discontented with the status quo
but unable to do anything about it.

IMBOLC

CARD 2

Season SPRING

Keyword AWAKENING

Element FIRE

Month FEBRUARY

Week 2ND

Astrology AQUARIUS / TAURUS

THE IMAGE: *A figure stands in a small boat-shaped object floating on a sea of clouds. The figure, arms folded across the breast, forms the trunk of a young tree in full leaf. The clouds symbolize the air sign Aquarius and the intellect. The tree figure is the gradually awakening earth sign Taurus.*

The second Imbolc card brings the nature of the sign Taurus into partnership with the Sun's current sign Aquarius. Taurus is slow to move into action and, unlike Aries, will not do this prematurely. Only in the state of being fully awake and aware will this cautious sign take action. This way mistakes are rarely made and the potential for future development has a solid ground to grow on. Restless Aquarius finds a slower partner can be soothing and helpful in giving time to thought and planning – at which the inventive water-carrier excels. Ideas that are formulated by this combination at this time are usually well founded and without too much risk; this card indicates a well-considered venture. The two signs are, however, not the most compatible – sparky Aquarius the revolutionary and Taurus the gentle pleasure-loving stick-in-the-mud – so sometimes the awakening can take an infuriatingly long time. The result, however, is usually worth the wait.

IN A READING

Catching on to a new idea slowly. A careful start to a new venture.
Cautiously entering into a new partnership. The attraction of opposites.
Surprise that you are attracted to someone eccentric.
Gradually coming around to a new point of view.
Being forced to think an idea out sensibly.
Having to restrain yourself from 'going the whole hog' with something.

WHEN REVERSED

Feeling worried about the negative aspects of a new project.
Having someone lose interest in your ideas.
Being seduced into something rash.
A relationship which no longer has any sparkle.
Being put off by someone else's overenthusiasm.
Being lulled into a false sense of security by a smooth talker.

IMBOLC

CARD 3

Season SPRING
Keyword INSIGHT
Element FIRE
Month FEBRUARY
Week 3RD
Astrology AQUARIUS / GEMINI

THE IMAGE: *Supporting a great winged all-seeing eye are the head and shoulders of a serene meditating woman. At her neck is the collar of authority decorated with the elemental cross and a teardrop. Three figures kneel below, hands raised in anticipation of the words of the oracle.*

The third week of spring is the last one ruled by the Aquarius Sun, and here it is partnered harmoniously with another air sign, Gemini. Air signs express themselves through sociable communication and intellect. This card indicates a great deal of discussion and insight brought to bear on the current question. Both signs excel in sharp perception and breadth of knowledge, providing a strong intellectual response to any mental challenge. Aquarius is the questioner and lateral thinker, and Gemini is the researcher. The two are a formidable combination. This card indicates a sociable time when there will be many friends available for advice and shared thoughts – a talking rather than an acting period, when good perceptive thought saves a lot of unnecessary rushing around. These two signs are strong in education and communicative matters, and may indicate that going back to college and restudying a subject will be beneficial. This combination will produce inventiveness and innovation. It has the potential to see through past mistakes and deliver the appropriate answers for the current situation.

IN A READING

A revealing piece of information. Taking professional advice.
A discussion that helps to make something clear.
Being helped by a well-informed acquaintance.
Reading up on a subject that you may get involved with later.
Preparing to make a job application.
Attaching yourself to someone as if they were a guru or philosophical teacher.

WHEN REVERSED

A mental block. Failure to understand the current situation.
Taking bad or unhelpful advice.
Being unable to acquire the necessary information in order to move on.
Coming up against someone who refuses to understand your point of view.

IMBOLC

CARD 4

Season SPRING

Keyword CHILDHOOD

Element FIRE

Month FEBRUARY

Week 4TH

Astrology PISCES / CANCER

THE IMAGE: *A centred Celtic circle is surrounded by four childlike figures who, with their hands linked and their hair entwined, make the diagonal cross of Gyfu. They give the impression that they are rotating around the Celtic circle. Above and below are two decorative panels representing water, emotions and the two water signs Cancer and Pisces.*

I n the fourth week of February the Sun moves into Pisces which combines with the fourth sign, Cancer. This is the period when young creatures begin to frisk and play, expressing new-found movement and a sense of self. Both Pisces and Cancer are water signs and relate strongly to emotional matters. The Piscean nature is able to empathize with the hopes and fears of others in an almost clairvoyant way. The Cancerian is the archetypal caring, sensitive and devoted mother. At this time, the year is in its childhood; it is growing and needs nurturing and protecting. During this period family concerns and responsibilities may come to the fore. This is, however, a happy card and is likely to describe a time when you become a child again, when you throw off adult inhibitions and give in to spontaneous play. With the Pisces Sun there will be a need to indulge imaginative abilities and to tap into the feelings of, and be at one with, those who are younger and less experienced. Cancer, whose role is usually the parent, reverses their part and becomes a carefree youngster forgetting the cares of the world.

IN A READING

Being put into a position where you happily feel as a child again.
A feeling of being looked after by someone. Letting your hair down.
A sudden revelation that you have been missing something.
A strong memory of childhood is aroused.
A friend from your childhood comes back into your life.

WHEN REVERSED

Being treated as if you're not yet an adult.
Someone has made you feel foolish or embarrassed.
Feeling that you aren't ready for something that is offered to you.
A feeling that you have lost something.

IMBOLC

CARD 5

Season SPRING

Keyword PLANS

Element FIRE

Month MARCH

Week 1ST

Astrology PISCES / LEO

THE IMAGE: *In a rose-tinted sky, a kilted figure with arms and legs outstretched is splayed on a spinning five-pointed star. At each point of the star hangs a smaller, unidentifiable figure enjoying the ride. Below is a landscape with a path that curves around a hill out of sight.*

This card is ruled by the fifth zodiac sign, Leo, and during the first week of March the Sun is still passing through Pisces. This is a combination of creative fire and emotional water. The Leo ability to see a blank canvas and know exactly what to paint on it is irrepressible and this, combined with the psychic Pisces talents, leads to a host of plans and designs for the future. This represents a time when ideas and plans of all kinds, especially large scale (Leo), will take on more importance. There will almost be a feeling that the storming of ideas creates an excitement and pleasure in its own right, and it matters little whether they turn into something more tangible. Whatever the project, it will be necessary to call in someone a little more practical to help get the best of the ideas into action. Leo is a big thinker but the royal lion always needs a willing servant to assist him. Pisces is a dreamer and more often than not sees the vision as reality and leaves it at that. So all in all, ideas flow fast at this time but the message is to settle on one and make it reality.

IN A READING

Having a planning session. A desire to turn a lifelong dream into a reality.
Being carried along on someone else's ideas.
Being overpowered by too many plans and getting nothing done.
Putting ambitions firmly on the agenda.
A danger of overenthusiasm giving away a good idea
for someone more practical to exploit.

WHEN REVERSED

Having your ideas rejected. Listlessness and lack of ambition.
Finding yourself in a position where you can't look ahead.
Being at someone else's beck and call and having no say in the matter.

6   IMBOLC   △

ℋ℡ | MARCH 2ND WEEK CLEANSING | 🌱

IMBOLC

CARD 6

Season SPRING

Keyword CLEANSING

Element FIRE

Month MARCH

Week 2ND

Astrology PISCES / VIRGO

THE IMAGE: *A luminous figure of a woman surrounded by an aura is framed by her golden hair and two budding plants. The seven chakras in their seven colours are marked down her body. Either side of her head are two whirling circles of energy.*

All number six cards are ruled by the sixth sign Virgo, and in the spring suit it is Sun-ruled by the opposite sign Pisces. Traditionally, Virgo is concerned with dutiful service and, above all, health issues. Virgo is devoted to achieving comfortable perfection in the material world, and Pisces with perfection in the spiritual world. So although these two signs are opposites, they are complementary. The idea of cleansing expressed here, when related to the runic year is in preparation for the flowering phase ahead. Like a garden where the first shoots of spring have proliferated and everywhere is a mass of intertwined shoots and leaves growing where they will, there is now some need for order. Small, delicate plants must be given space, failing plants must be pulled out, and all must be prepared, with loving care, for future growth. In the same way, we need to care for our own well-being. We must clear the clutter that gathers so easily around us, and the bad habits we are always about to give up, and set up a sensible health regime to enrich our life and improve our progress.

IN A READING

Starting a new health and fitness regime. Giving up a bad habit.
Changing your lifestyle drastically. Following a new spiritual path.
An attraction to alternative philosophies, both physical and spiritual.
Clearing away some of the 'dead wood' in your life. A make-over.
Taking on a new job in a caring or alternative health company.

WHEN REVERSED

Neglecting your health. Living an excessive and overindulgent lifestyle.
Being unable to give up bad habits.
A negative experience with alternative medicine.
Feeling disappointed in yourself for failing to keep up a health regime.

IMBOLC

CARD 7

Season SPRING
Keyword SYMPATHY
Element FIRE
Month MARCH
Week 3RD
Astrology PISCES / LIBRA

THE IMAGE: *Two beautiful women caress each other – one young and one older. They are well cared for and each offers the other a gift: the young girl offers vitality and youth; the older woman offers love and experience. They are the feminine side in all of us.*

In the third week of March, the Sun moves through the last degrees of Pisces. The seventh card of spring is of the nature of Libra. The keywords of these two signs define sensitivity (Pisces) within close relationships (Libra). Libra is an air sign and is primarily concerned with partnership issues. With this sign there is always an ability to see the other person's point of view, making this a particularly powerful combination for helping others in times of distress. This card can appear both when sympathy is needed for yourself, and when others need your sensitive and wholehearted support. The qualities of diplomacy and balance in Libra suggest that the support can manifest as strong argument and defence of a position. Often, this card will show when there is a legal argument to be made, and it may indicate sympathetic but practical support to put right an injustice. Pisces has the emotional resilience to take on unlimited amounts of other people's problems, sharing the burden equally for as long as it is necessary. There is a slight danger with this card that you may not be able to remain detached enough to give the best support.

IN A READING

Being, or needing, a shoulder to cry on. The need to share a burden.
Giving practical support to someone in difficulty.
Taking a positive action with regard to a good cause.
Speaking up for someone who has been maligned or put down in some way.
Publicizing an injustice and gathering support.

WHEN REVERSED

Being refused sympathy and left to bear a difficult situation alone.
Having an unsympathetic and uncaring decision made against you.
Losing a close relationship. An argument leading to a family rift.

8   IMBOLC   △

MARCH 4TH WEEK
CHALLENGE

IMBOLC
CARD 8

Season SPRING

Keyword CHALLENGE

Element FIRE

Month MARCH

Week 4TH

Astrology ARIES / SCORPIO

THE IMAGE: *A sky dragon with forked tongue grimaces and prepares itself for battle. Its scales are like armour and its tongue and tail like arrowheads. The landscape curls and writhes to mirror the dragon's aggressive movement.*

The eighth card of each suit is ruled by the powerful water sign Scorpio, and in the fourth week of March the Sun moves into the fire sign Aries. This is a transforming month with a Martian feel as both signs are ruled by the action planet Mars. It is about self-assertion and the courage to tackle anything and everything. They have the same attitude to anything that dares challenge this fiery nature. With Scorpio there is an extreme desire to get down to basics; all dead wood must be rooted out and space made for clear movement. Aries, the all-action ideal partner, will surge ahead and lead the way. This card represents challenge and transformation. Something has to be dealt with, and quickly. There is no hanging back; all the essentials for success are on hand. Heroes and heroines think not of failure; they just act. Aries and Scorpio are both resilient, and when wounded they have the power to recuperate and become better than they were before. So failure or success matters little, but what has to be done must be done.

IN A READING

Deciding to face something rather than run.
Being prepared to go into battle for the sake of upholding a belief.
Finding a new strength at the right moment. Confidence in your own success.
Desiring or setting up a new challenge, in order to break out
of a dull and meaningless period in your life.

WHEN REVERSED

Taking the coward's way out and running away from a difficult problem.
Projecting your own aggression onto someone else.
Getting someone else to do your dirty work.
Leaving a partner when things get difficult.
Being the victim of violence or aggression.

IMBOLC
CARD 9

Season SPRING
Keyword ACTIVITY
Element FIRE
Month APRIL
Week 1ST
Astrology ARIES / SAGITTARIUS

THE IMAGE: *Through a garden arch two peasant figures carrying the tools of their labours move actively about their business. Above the arch small shoots are growing. It is a scene of the hard work necessary to nurture and maintain the beautiful garden.*

Two fire signs combine to make an all-action significator in this card. In the first week of April the Sun is in the sign Aries, known as the pioneer of the zodiac, and with the ninth card being ruled by Sagittarius we have the explorer. This time of the year is filled with the hustle and bustle of things to get done and pleasure to be enjoyed. For these two signs, hard work is the greatest pleasure. This card represents throwing yourself into an overload of hard work and absolutely loving it. Maybe this is a new partnership that has engendered a new vitality and enthusiasm for life. Perhaps there is just a great feeling of well-being and energy within you that needs to be well occupied. With this much fire, things are highly competitive. There will be moments when tempers fray, and a little too much heat can sometimes set sparks flying. Quarrels can be fierce but are rarely long lasting. The Sagittarian influence of the card can sometimes inadvertently lead to a tactless blunder but, generally, this is a good-natured and hearty time.

IN A READING

Strong determination is shown, which can indicate
a powerful competition of some kind.
A large amount of important chores to be worked through.
Clearing out in preparation for the next phase of a project.
A quarrel in the heat of the moment. Much energy is available for a project.

WHEN REVERSED

Not being able to keep up with others at work.
Being left with a large burden because of others' laziness.
Being outdone by someone with whom you are in competition.
Interference in your work.
A project fails or is cancelled and a great deal of energy is wasted.

IMBOLC
CARD 10

Season SPRING
Keyword SELF-PROMOTION
Element FIRE
Month APRIL
Week 2ND
Astrology ARIES / CAPRICORN

THE IMAGE: *A colourful figure in a rune-decorated costume with a magnificent headdress moves across a field blowing on a horn. Figures in the distance wave in recognition and friendly greeting. The grass is patterned with small fire triangles of creativity.*

In the second week of April the Sun settles down on its path through Aries. This is the time when the lambs are gambolling and new life is everywhere, frisky and full of energy. The number ten card has Capricorn as its ruler, and this ambitious earth sign, signifying the public eye, will need to broadcast its existence to the world. The fullness of spring is everywhere. All new growth is established and well into its journey through the season. Capricorn respects the rules and is able to keep the wild and impulsive Aries well directed and on a straight track. But however sensible the materialistic Capricorn is, it can't resist a sense of pride in the achievements made so far. It knows when the time is ripe to stake claims and make known its possessions and position in the world. This is a time when there is strength in publicity and it is good to show our power in order to keep danger at bay. Capricorn is the shepherd with his flute and bell, warning the prowling wolves that the daring and impulsive young lambs are not for them.

IN A READING

A warning given against a possible threat.
A show of strength through prestige and your position in an organization.
Using your position to protect the less capable.
Setting up a good system as an example to others.
Putting yourself forward for an important position.
Blowing your own trumpet.

WHEN REVERSED

Being on the wrong end of some bad publicity.
Having a derogatory rumour spread about you.
A failure to get noticed on an important occasion.
Not respecting your own abilities enough to speak up for yourself.
A shrinking violet. Being blacklisted.

IMBOLC

CARD 11

Season SPRING
Keyword RECKLESSNESS
Element FIRE
Month APRIL
Week 3RD
Astrology ARIES / AQUARIUS

THE IMAGE: *On top of a strange stone borie (a dry-stone igloo-like hut) painted with coloured animal figures kneels a naked girl. Around the stone twines a serpent with its head facing the girl. She stretches an open hand towards the strange beast in friendly affection.*

The third week of April sees the exaltation of the Sun in Aries. Eleven is the number of Aquarius, and here we have the almost dangerous combination of the oddball and the impulsive. Aries ruled by impetuous Mars and Aquarius by eccentric Uranus are a wild combination. It is as if the lambs are turning into young rams, and are testing their new-found confidence and strength against all and sundry. This is a time when impulsive, adventurous lambs become lunch for the waiting wolves. On the other hand, this card may tell us to be bold – there is no other way to grow than to test your abilities. Sometimes we need to feel danger in order to fully understand what it is, and to be able to cope when fate throws us into real danger. There comes a moment when all of us, feeling overprotected in some way, wish to try something on our own despite what others say. This card is the essence of bold fire and air at work, and it is expressed as fast ideas and immediate action – thrilling and risky.

IN A READING

Giving in to a mad impulse. A wild and impossible love affair.
Signing up for an adventure trip. Testing your strength.
Bluffing your way into a deal with the danger of being discovered.
Risking something of great value on a sudden whim.
An attempt to turn over a traditional way of doing things
for something outrageously new.

WHEN REVERSED

Feeling terrified of taking an opportunity when the outcome is uncertain.
Missing out on something because you were too cautious.
Regretfully choosing the straight and narrow path.
Going for the safe relationship rather than the wickedly exciting one.

IMBOLC
CARD 12

Season SPRING
Keyword SATISFACTION
Element FIRE
Month APRIL
Week 4TH
Astrology TAURUS / PISCES

THE IMAGE: *A regal-looking man stands facing us. In one hand he holds a sceptre surmounted by a Celtic cross. In the other hand he plays with a knotted curl. On his shoulder is a sphinx. He is richly dressed and has a look of great satisfaction.*

In the fourth week of April the Sun gives himself a rest in the pleasure-loving sign of Taurus. Just so that the boat isn't rocked, the ruler of spring card twelve is gentle, understanding Pisces. What a pleasant card of great satisfaction. This is the time of year between spring and summer when Taurus's senses of touch, smell and taste are entering the indulgent phase. The countryside smells sweet, is a rich green and is beginning to allow its buds to burst into the first tiny blossoms. It represents a period when things are running as they should be: there is a warm feeling of expectation and the pace of life slows down, allowing us enough time to sit back a little and enjoy it. Taurus is the great nurturer of things small that can grow into things vast and useful. They are the builders and gardeners of this planet and their pace is slow. Tree-planters are not in the hurry that pioneering Arians are. Life is not just about getting things done well; it is also about taking time off to realize our good fortune – time for a little Taurean sensuality combined with Piscean daydreaming.

IN A READING

Time to take a well-earned rest after a long working period.
Indulging your dreams in flights of fancy. A long holiday.
Spending some time on yourself for a change.
Being in a position where you can profitably exploit your good taste.
Moving into work where other people's comfort and well-being are involved.

WHEN REVERSED

Overindulgence and self-satisfaction.
Being on the receiving end of someone's overbearing conceit.
Acting boastfully with little reason.
Suffering a great disappointment after high expectations.

SUMMER SOLSTICE

*Sun in Cancer on
or around 21 June*

This is the day when the Sun enters the first water sign Cancer. The word 'Solstice' is derived from the two Latin words 'sol' (sun) and 'sistere' (to cause to stand still). This is the longest day of the Sun's light and the magic of the solar orb is at its height. At the annual celebrations sun – or fire – wheels are ignited and rolled down hillsides. Great bonfires are lit at the highest points across the country. It remains, of course, one of the most significant festivals of the druids, and their annual presence at the ancient site of Stonehenge is still important. This happy time of year, between the planting and harvesting of the crops, was traditionally the most popular month for weddings. This is due to the belief that the union of the goddess and god occurred at Beltane and, therefore, it was a time of great fertility. The June full moon was always known as the 'honey moon' as this was found to be the most profitable time to harvest the honey from the beehives. It is said that newlyweds were offered dishes containing this excellent honey for the first month of their marriage, to enhance their chances of fertility, hence the honeymoon and the desire to be June brides that still prevails. In the idea of marriage and the hopes for offspring, we find the concept of the sign Cancer and its association with marriage, parenthood and family. It speaks of emotions, fertility and the blossoming of the earth mother herself. This is the Earth in full flower and is presented to the world with pride.

IN A READING

Look at the other cards in the reading and see what is implied by those that are close by. This strong card will affect the other cards greatly, indicating that despite other conditions a presentation of your talents will be essential if you are to see a positive outcome. It signifies a time when you must be bold and what you have to show must be honestly revealed.

BELTANE

CARD 1

Season SUMMER

Keyword ENTERPRISE

Element WATER

Month MAY

Week 1ST

Astrology TAURUS / ARIES

THE IMAGE: *A tower rises up to the sky. It is crowned by a great Celtic cross, around which ribbons are entwined as on the traditional maypole. Figures dance around the tower, climbing higher and higher as they go. The ladders, which symbolize ambition, assist the climb.*

In the first week of May the Sun moves through Taurus, and being the number one card in the summer cycle, Aries is co-ruler. This is a combination of enterprises, where the sensible and cautious business mind of Taurus gets an extra nudge from go-getting Aries. This is not without a little friction; there is potential for a stalemate situation, when the irresistible force meets the immovable object. Happily, both signs like to see tangible results, and the Taurean need to build on past efforts and the Arien muscle are enough to make the most of this colourful season. It is an optimistic time for those who work hard, and the 1 May celebration has always been dedicated to the workers of the land. In ancient times the Celts and Saxons celebrated 1 May, Beltane, as the day of fire. Bel, the Celtic god of the Sun, was revered at this welcome return of warmth and fertility to the soil. The Druids supervised and organized the lighting of the Beltane fires which were taken to each house to rekindle the household fires that had been extinguished in preparation for this long-awaited and cleansed new light.

IN A READING

The beginning of a new enterprise. An unlikely, but profitable, partnership.
Producing something for the comfort of others.
A male/female business partnership.
A good time for setting up horticultural or fashion projects.
Being pushed into a new project that you are slightly reluctant about.
Finding a new partner with whom you can progress your ambitions.

WHEN REVERSED

A job or business opportunity that passes you by.
Finding life a difficult, uphill struggle.
Seeing yourself passed over for promotion in favour of those you think less able.
Resisting the possibility of a positive change out of laziness.

BELTANE

CARD 2

Season SUMMER

Keyword APPRECIATION

Element WATER

Month MAY

Week 2ND

Astrology TAURUS / TAURUS

THE IMAGE: *A beautiful woman dressed as a queen with a crown gazes at her reflection in a mirror. She sees not her face but a beautiful lotus flower. It is an image of self-worth and an appreciation of beauty.*

All number two cards are ruled by the second sign Taurus, and as this is also the sign where the Sun is placed this week we have a double Taurus emphasis. Taurus is probably the most sensual and appreciative sign in the zodiac and, as here these qualities are directed at itself, we have a lot of self-satisfaction showing in the meaning of this card. For a short while this shows a feel-good frame of mind. It is a card that may or may not have sexual overtones, but seasonally it represents the summer feeling good about itself. Flowers are in bloom, the birds are singing, the air is fresh and the world is basking in the Sun. What more can you want? It is, however, also a time when we can prove to be somewhat overindulgent, lethargic and self-satisfied in the extreme. Sometimes guilt can set in if we feel that we are too proud of the results of our efforts, but maybe we need not feel so badly about it when we see the fruits of our labours looking so good. It's a pat on the back and a short break before getting on with the demands of the season.

IN A READING

Taking a much-needed break.
Indulging in a little boasting about past achievements.
Putting on a show or display, either for business or reputation.
Gaining an award or recognition of some kind.
Giving yourself a long-awaited make-over.
Spoiling yourself with a little Taurean-style extravagance –
jewellery, new clothes, a new apartment, an expensive holiday.

WHEN REVERSED

Not recognizing your own abilities and self-worth.
Acting or speaking in a self-effacing manner through shyness.
Being careless or even slovenly with your appearance.
Trying not to be noticed in case it puts a demand on you.

BELTANE

CARD 3

Season SUMMER

Keyword NEGOTIATION

Element WATER

Month MAY

Week 3RD

Astrology TAURUS / GEMINI

THE IMAGE: *Two hands reach towards each other in agreement. Each extends from a richly embroidered sleeve denoting power. Around the meeting hands the symbols of property, achievement and the rune Feoh – meaning movable wealth – give their influence to the negotiators.*

The third week of May sees the Sun moving through the last few degrees of Taurus, and card number three is ruled by Gemini. This is an excellent combination for negotiation and all kinds of correspondence concerned with acquiring or selling property. Taurus is the sign that governs our possessions, including our abilities or talents which are seen as something we own. Gemini deals with all kinds of mental work and verbal communication. These two together indicate the need for much discussion in order to come to an agreement about the acquisition of possessions or the products of our labours. This, in ancient country life, would have been typified by the bartering and back-and-forth negotiation necessary to exchange produce for other goods. This was the natural way of ancient agricultural communities, and expectations of the harvest later in the year would be subject to much haggling. The planets ruling the two signs are Venus and Mercury, so this card can also indicate the other meaning of Venus, relationships. At this time marriages of daughters and sons and dowries would be arranged.

IN A READING

The signing of a contract. Negotiation of a business deal.
Acquisition of a new piece of property. An arranged marriage.
A mercenary relationship formed just for convenience.
Successfully asking for a pay rise at work.
Plucking up the courage to ask someone that attracts you for a date.

WHEN REVERSED

A contract that is broken. The failure of a relationship.

BELTANE

CARD 4

Season SUMMER
Keyword TRADITION
Element WATER
Month MAY
Week 4TH
Astrology GEMINI/CANCER

THE IMAGE: *A stone figure inscribed with runes that symbolizes ancestors, stands as a precious monument to the family. Around the solid, impressive carving a small family make their ritual offerings to the past to ensure the unbroken line and the secure continuation of their traditions.*

The Sun moves into Gemini in the last week of May, and the number four card is strongly influenced by Cancer. This symbolizes the passing on of family traditions. Gemini, with its ruler Mercury, implies links, communication and the recording of information, while Moon-ruled Cancer shows family and past experience. Here we have the powerful force that unites us with our roots. Although during our youth, to assert our individuality, we all go through a period of rebellion where families are concerned, gradually the history and the knowledge that has been passed on to us seeps back into our system and we become the sum total of our newly gained experience and our inherited family ways. This card, in the symbolism of the agricultural life, is the passing on from generation to generation of the crafts and country lore that enables the smooth rhythmic running of rural life. With maturity comes the knowledge that much of that which has been passed down to us by our ancestors is of timeless value. Even partaking in seemingly useless rituals becomes a precious and necessary link with our inheritance. In this card we value our roots and the continuation of the successful regeneration that has been occurring since the beginning of time.

IN A READING

Listening to the advice of an elder. An occasion that unites family members.
Work involving history, perhaps relating to archaeology, antiques or museums.
Links with distant relatives. Carrying on a family occupation.
An interest in genealogy and keeping family records. Learning an old craft.

WHEN REVERSED

Being hampered by your old, outdated ways.
Finding that family ties are holding you back from achieving success.
Doing something because it is expected of you rather than because you want to.
A traditional family gathering that has outgrown its pleasure.

5	BELTANE	▽

June 1st week
CONCEPT

BELTANE

CARD 5

Season SUMMER

Keyword CONCEPT

Element WATER

Month JUNE

Week 1ST

Astrology GEMINI/LEO

THE IMAGE: *The calm face on the Sun's golden orb is surrounded by flames that resemble the flowing mane of the lion. This is Leo, the sign of creativity and vision. The great solar king passes a scroll to the brightly coloured Geminian bird about to take flight.*

All number five cards are ruled by the fifth sign Leo, and, since in this suit the card falls in the first week of June, it is Sun-ruled by Gemini. Leo is the big planner of the zodiac and Gemini is the brain. This combination has the ability to see the whole picture of any situation rather than the separate parts. On a large scale, Leo can stand back and get a good view of the way ahead. Mercurial Gemini's quick and ever-curious mind picks up enough all-round information to put together a cohesive plan. This is the part of the yearly cycle when the careful preparation that has been done shows results, and thoughts can be turned to the future. It is a time when new ideas and fresh approaches to what has become a repeat pattern can be indulged and developed. Nothing can be allowed to stagnate, but the thought must come before the act. Sound and imaginative vision are the meaning of this card.

IN A READING

A brainstorming session to plan for the future. A far-seeing piece of advice.
Presenting a brilliant idea to someone who may help with its realization.
A flight of fancy that may become a possibility as time goes by.
Gaining the respect of others through your perceptive thinking.

WHEN REVERSED

A project that fails, making it necessary to go back to the drawing board.
Someone passing off your ideas as their own.
Dabbling in too many ideas and completing none.
A Jack of all trades and master of none.

6	BELTANE	▽

| ♊♍ | JUNE 2ND WEEK ANALYSIS | ❀ |

BELTANE
CARD 6

Season SUMMER
Keyword ANALYSIS
Element WATER
Month JUNE
Week 2ND
Astrology GEMINI / VIRGO

THE IMAGE: *A woman supports a decorative plinth containing two birds, a book and a quill – symbols of thought, writing, education and imagination. In the centre above her head is the earth cross, representing the balance of the four elements fire, earth, air and water.*

The second week of June with the Sun in Gemini joins here with the Virgo influences of the sixth card. Following the fifth card with the keyword 'concept', the issue is put under the scrutiny of the zodiac's number one researcher, Virgo. Plans must be analysed and dissected in order to ascertain their viability. The razor-sharp, quicksilver-thinking planet Mercury rules both Gemini and Virgo. Between the two no thought is left unconsidered. This is the natural editing team of the zodiac in harness, symbolized by the dead-heading of the first flowers to make room for the next blooms. Trimming back the surplus twisting shoots of the vine allows the strong fruit-bearing ones a full and rich growth. This can be a time of infuriating niggles and nit-picking but always in the knowledge that the rewards will be worth having. It is a period that requires devotion to the job in hand and unlimited patience. With this combination there is also a strong tendency to gather research and information, almost for the sheer pleasure of it.

IN A READING

A long period of research for a project. Contact with a perfectionist.
Having to compile a report of some kind.
Helping a younger person with schoolwork.
Learning a useful new technology for work. Going on a course.
An interest in reading – and learning – about health matters.

WHEN REVERSED

Coming under severe criticism for something you have prepared.
Being subjected to an unwanted examination.
Giving in to temptation and breaking a health regime.
Being the subject of gossip and bad publicity.
A rejection letter from a job application.
Needlessly accepting second best for yourself.

BELTANE

CARD 7

Season SUMMER
Keyword GATHERING
Element WATER
Month JUNE
Week 3RD
Astrology GEMINI / LIBRA

THE IMAGE: *A table is spread with food and drink for a gathering. The tablecloth is patterned with traditional designs and the guests are dressed in their finery to suit the occasion. It is a simple but light-hearted scene of social enjoyment where conversation and gossip flow and laughter prevails.*

Two air signs combine in the third week of June to bring a sociable last few days of the Sun's passage through Gemini. Libra is primarily concerned with harmonious and pleasing relationships of all kinds, and Gemini represents the gossips and news gatherers that keep the conversation sparkling. The days are longer and the evenings lighter, allowing more time for pleasure during this warm and friendly month. It is a period of plenty and the natural impulse is to share the summer's bounty. Work isn't high on the agenda and making and remaking friendships becomes all important. The summer Sun calls us to gather in large groups at holiday resorts, giving ourselves to the warmth of our great star and each other's joyful company. This is a time for short-term and not-too-serious flirtatiousness, as the planets ruling these two signs are Mercury and Venus. Youth and beauty are foremost but the more mature are also susceptible to the heady perfume of summer gardens. It is a holiday time when romance is in the air.

IN A READING

A busy social calendar with many visits to and from friends.
A long-awaited holiday. A housewarming.
A brief love affair or holiday romance. Sharing a love of beautiful things.
Being in the company of like-minded friends.
Making arrangements for a big social event.
Helping a friend make an important decision.

WHEN REVERSED

A dreaded social event that you feel obliged to attend.
Being embarrassed and made to feel guilty by the generosity of neglected friends.
Losing the companionship of old friends through a change of circumstances.
A social occasion organized by you that becomes a disaster.

BELTANE

CARD 8

Season SUMMER

Keyword PROTECTION

Element WATER

Month JUNE

Week 4TH

Astrology CANCER / SCORPIO

THE IMAGE: *A crowned angel holds a child protectively. She is the great mother symbolized in the nurturing qualities of the sign Cancer. The disc of the Sun halos the angel's head. In the crown is an eye that watches for potential dangers to her precious charge.*

With the fourth week of June at the Summer Solstice, the Sun moves into the sign of Cancer – the crab. It is joined in the eighth card by another watery sign, Scorpio the scorpion, and here we have an emotional duo that are in sympathetic rapport. Both creatures symbolically defend and protect, and it is second nature for them to predict, and be prepared for, any unforeseen danger. This card implies that things are too good to last, so although life is to be enjoyed to the full we must also keep an eye open for any unexpected occurrences that may rock the boat. At times when everything seems perfect we can become complacent and vulnerable to the foibles of fate. The eight card of summer represents the part in all of us that instinctively has an ear cocked against potential disaster. It is the mother creature and her new brood that are a constant pleasure and, inevitably, a constant worry. It is a sacrificing combination, for in order that their charges are able to enjoy life in joyful and exuberant freedom, the protector is never able to abandon their responsibilities and share fully in the pleasure.

IN A READING

Taking out some kind of insurance. Help from a mother.
Someone acting in an overprotective manner towards you.
Fighting against oppressive or unwelcome attention.
Going to the aid of someone you feel responsible for.
Giving guidance to a younger or more inexperienced person.

WHEN REVERSED

Feeling that you need protection from a threatening person or situation.
Being seduced into thinking that someone has your
best interests at heart when this isn't true.
Someone trying to save their own skin by blaming you.

BELTANE
CARD 9

Season SUMMER
Keyword CELEBRATION
Element WATER
Month JULY
Week 1ST
Astrology CANCER / SAGITTARIUS

THE IMAGE: *A trio of musicians and entertainers dance along an earthy road accompanied by a child. They are dressed in festive costumes and the atmosphere is carefree and full of gaiety. They are the performers for a celebration.*

The Sun in the summer sign Cancer, and card nine Sagittarius, make for a water–fire combination. There is an irrepressible optimism that the Archer's ruling planet Jupiter engenders. The Moon-ruled Cancer here is on an emotional high – all is well with the world, let's party! This is a combination that produces great enthusiasm for life and a desire to explore the pleasure of a celebration. Usually this is in the form of a period of self-congratulation, after the successful conclusion of a long spell of hard work. As Jupiter is the largest of all our planets, all Jovian influences symbolize growth, expansion and even some excessive indulgence. As the nature of most celebrations is a little too much too often, there can be regrets later but mostly the effect is beneficial. Cancer is a great traditionalist, and makes the most of yearly family and social occasions. Often, this card will indicate happy and renewed contacts with those living far away. It can also show some kind of educational achievement.

IN A READING

Celebrating winning an award or achieving an educational qualification.
A generous present from a woman. An important family occasion.
Being with a large group or organization that has
the same ideals, philosophy or beliefs.
Following the opinions of those you respect.

WHEN REVERSED

Being made to feel unwelcome at a family or social celebration.
A celebration that is premature and regretted as the reason for its being fades.
A period of overindulgence that is later regretted.
Trying to put a brave face on matters for the sake of others
when you feel least like it.

BELTANE
CARD 10

Season SUMMER
Keyword RESPONSIBILITY
Element WATER
Month JULY
Week 2ND
Astrology CANCER / CAPRICORN

THE IMAGE: *On a green field a capable and devoted earth mother gives birth to a child. Seated on her knees are two older children. Her children are of many colours and are contented and well cared for. The life blood flows through her fertile body and provides energy and sustenance for her offspring.*

In the second week of July the Sun moves through Cancer. The ruler of card number ten is Capricorn, the opposite sign in the circle of the zodiac. Whereas Cancer refers to our home and family needs, Capricorn is our responsibility and position with regard to society as a whole. This is where we conform to the rules and regulations that enable the smooth running of our everyday life. We keep a balance between what we need to take to support ourselves and what we have to give back in return. This, in the early agricultural communities, was the way of the countryside, where due respect was paid to the needs of the earth, the creatures and the crops. So with present-day life, we pay our taxes and contribute to the provision of maintenance for our towns and countryside. This card represents the cycle of finding a partner, having a family and the extra responsibility that incurs. It may, in extreme cases, become a case of 'keeping up with the Joneses', but it is a mature and generally considerate message, nevertheless.

IN A READING

Strong emphasis on growing family duties. The birth of a baby.
Taking a position in the local community. Being elected to public office.
Adopting a child. Involvement in social work.
Looking after parents or older relatives. Working in a position of trust.
Inheriting or taking over a family business.

WHEN REVERSED

Being overwhelmed by extra duties at work.
Suddenly being selected for an important job
that you aren't sure you can manage.
Feeling unable to cope with a new family situation.

11 BELTANE ▽

JULY 3RD WEEK
BREAKING TRADITION

BELTANE

CARD 11

Season SUMMER

Keyword BREAKING TRADITION

Element WATER

Month JULY

Week 3RD

Astrology CANCER / AQUARIUS

THE IMAGE: *A strange, half-mermaid figure (but winged instead of finned) floats in the air. Far below is a gentle, green, undulating landscape. Entwined around the arms of the figure are two winged, birdlike serpents that carry her high above the earth.*

In direct contrast to the previous card, here we have the influence of the lateral thinking and rebelling sign Aquarius. Combining with the Sun in Cancer in the third week of July, it takes a new look at traditional ways of doing things – and usually rejects them. Sometimes this is contrariness designed to spark off new awareness and set others thinking and talking. This combination of Moon-ruled Cancer and Uranus-ruled

Aquarius is electric, and represents those who have a radical approach to family life and the education of children. The nature of Aquarius is humanitarian and open to the new and innovative. This, counterbalanced by the sensitive and caring ways of Cancer, makes for leadership in fights for good causes and the rights for those less fortunate in life. This card indicates individuals who don't accept all at face value, but examine and try other ways to see if improvements can be made. It is as necessary a function as that of conforming – represented by card ten – and prevents the yearly routine from becoming one of boredom and stagnation. It indicates that ways of the past that are still valued should stay, and those that are outdated and no longer working must go.

IN A READING

A new approach to family routine. A house move.
A new job working for a caring organization. Fighting for a good cause.
Breaking a routine that has become nothing but a habit.
Rethinking your attitude to life. Joining an alternative philosophy group.
Doing something out of character as an experiment.

WHEN REVERSED

Behaving in an outrageous or eccentric manner in order to gain attention.
Someone breaking a promise and acting contrary to expectations.
Being taken in by a fraud or a charlatan.
An irrepressible desire to throw everything to the winds.

BELTANE

CARD 12

Season SUMMER

Keyword VISION

Element WATER

Month JULY

Week 4TH

Astrology LEO / PISCES

THE IMAGE: *A serene tree goddess dreams, as if in a trance, and looks inward from above the branches that are part of her. The branches hold all facets of everyday life. A further pair of eyes, green and penetrating, stares out of the picture at the viewer.*

With the fourth week of July the Sun moves into its own sign Leo. It shares this card with the twelfth sign Pisces. This spells a future-orientated message. Leo signifies the ability to see a blank canvas and know just what the final picture will be; a big thinker with vision that makes the solar lion the most creative of all the signs. This, in combination with the dreamer–poet Pisces, produces a team that will set plans moving during this highly imaginative period. Leo is not an everyday worker, so any visualization conceived will need willing workers to assist his or her majesty to make the vision a reality. Pisces, too, is not the best finisher of the mundane details, and often the dream will suffice in its own right. However, this can be a time of brilliant ideas and forward-thinking. The Sun's powerful artistic and creative energies are unlimited, and with Neptune-ruled Pisces adding the most prolific imagination, this is a team of almost genius potential. Let's hope there are a couple of more practical signs around at this time to pick up the output and do something tangible with it.

IN A READING

A new, exciting contact with a creative group.
A dream with the possibility of a real outcome.
An excellent time to develop your creative talents.
An almost clairvoyant prediction of an event.
The ability to see potential in something that others feel is worthless.
A sudden attraction to someone that seems to have a future.

WHEN REVERSED

A premonition of something adverse.
Discovering that your brilliant idea has already been acted on by someone else.
Being unable to think clearly. Seeing your plans fail.
A difficulty in separating reality from fantasy.

ĀUTUMN EQUINOX

Sun in Libra on or around 23 September

Equinox means equal and night, and is the counterpoint of the Vernal or Spring Equinox when night and day are of the same length. At this time the Sun moves into the air sign Libra, meaning harmony and balance and indicating a time of great sociability. This is the period when the fruits of the earth are most prominent, leading to the celebration of the harvest. As the Spring Equinox was a time of great upsurge and new life, so the Autumn Equinox symbolizes a falling away; a gradual dying down and preparation for the winter rest. At the beginning of autumn the spring's new growth has reached full maturity. Small animals begin their preparation for winter, tree leaves turn to beautiful red and golden colours, and the air takes on a new chill. Most traditions consider this a time for harvesting crops and taking stock of the year's gain. It is also when we start to notice the lessening hours of daylight in anticipation of the Winter Solstice. As this time of year is one of the most temperate, it is considered a good time for reflection on the meaning of life. The traditional harvest festival, predating Christianity, was a feast that symbolically, and through sympathetic magic, called on the gods to ensure enough food and sustenance to last through the hard winter. Alban Elfed, a Druid festival to honour the Green Man, the god of the forest, was celebrated at this quarter day, which is one of the lesser Sabbats.

IN A READING

Look at nearby cards, as they will be influenced by this powerful card. It will enhance and add a note of optimism to even the most adverse cards and bring about a fruitful outcome. It signifies that whatever else is happening in the reading, this is a time for counting your blessings and putting some of your wares aside for the leaner times ahead.

LUGHNASADH
CARD 1

Season AUTUMN
Keywords RISK, GAMBLE
Element EARTH
Month AUGUST
Week 1ST
Astrology LEO / ARIES

THE IMAGE: *An antlered stag runs freely, not away from but alongside a leopard. These strange companions leap over the wheel of the Sun, sharing the exhilaration of their animal strength and matching each other with their speed.*

The Sun is moving through the fire sign Leo in the first week in August, and as the first card of autumn it shares its place with another – and the most impulsive – fire sign, Aries. There is so much heat in this combination that action is immediate, and can be unthinkingly premature. The card signifies risk and can have the qualities of extreme bravery or downright foolishness. It often shows a period when sheer nerve is demanded – the symbolism of the Ram and the Lion is not lacking in courage. In reality this can be expressed as a creative venture or enterprise, and the risk isn't necessarily physical. Nevertheless, it will require much determination and immediate action. This card may indicate a time when a quick and seemingly reckless decision must be made. To linger may be to lose all; to act may result in disaster. This is a time for the kind of madness that makes for heroism. The first card of Lughnasadh shows a partnership of like minds – adventurous and pioneering with potential for great achievements. This kind of action is never without its trials, and it is in the nature of this team that each failure sees them more determined to succeed.

IN A READING

An extreme gamble. Risking all on a whim.
Spontaneously going into partnership with someone
without background knowledge.
Throwing all you have into a project that you believe in.
Giving in to a sudden impulsive attraction.
A passionate, illicit or secret love affair. A financial gamble with property.

WHEN REVERSED

Being terrified to take the slightest risk in order to gain a great deal.
A huge loss through thoughtless actions.
A weakening of position or power. Mistrusting your partner.
Being deceived by someone selfish who only has their own desires in mind.

LUGHNASADH

CARD 2

Season AUTUMN
Keyword INVESTMENT
Element EARTH
Month AUGUST
Week 2ND
Astrology LEO / TAURUS

THE IMAGE: *A beautiful earth goddess, her head surmounted with sheaves of corn, wears a green ribbon and earth cross around her throat. The cross represents the four seasons, the four elements and the four cardinal points of the zodiac. Her arms are raised in approval.*

The number two card is ruled by Taurus, and in the second week of August it is accompanied by the Sun, which is still moving through Leo. Here, the fiery nature of Leo is tempered by the earthy and calmer nature of the Bull. Slow because time is necessary for small seeds to grow in the well-prepared ground, and with some kind of guarantee of future fruition, Taurus makes no move until the outcome is certain. Leo symbolizes the vision, the large-scale thinking of the venture and the life-giving warmth of inventive creativity. Taurus takes each stage at a gentle pace and rushes into nothing, but is confident at all times. These contrasting partners each contribute their own part of the investment. In rural life the collection and division of the Sun's produce provides grain for the miller's flour and seeds for next year's crops. This necessary balance is the measured and timeless husbandry of the earth. So with this card we are reminded that for any well-considered project to succeed we mustn't rush. Careful investment of both time and money is necessary for a successful outcome.

IN A READING

Coming to a stage when you need financial help in a venture.
Trying to work with someone or something that is slowing down progress.
Attempting to stop a partner from rushing into something
you are unsure about.
Receiving a windfall. An investment proves to have increased in value.

WHEN REVERSED

Getting into debt through extravagance and thoughtless behaviour.
Spending excessively to impress someone. The break-up of a partnership.
Being refused support for what you feel is a good project.
Having to take second place in an unequal partnership.

LUGHNASADH

CARD 3

Season AUTUMN

Keyword PUBLICITY

Element EARTH

Month AUGUST

Week 3RD

Astrology LEO / GEMINI

THE IMAGE: *An enormous stone floats mysteriously in the sky. On the stone a runic circle is engraved around a maze pattern. In the sky are constellations, and below in the landscape the trees have turned to autumn gold.*

The Sun moves through the last degrees of Leo and is combined with the ruler of the third card Gemini. The latter is the information source of the zodiac and, added to the fact that Leo has never been backward in letting the Sun's light shine for all to see, this is a card that puts the spotlight on publicity. This may be indicated quite literally, in the sense of the written word or a pamphlet advertising something. Or perhaps it will just be in letting the world know you're still around, and that it might be worth its while sitting up and taking a little notice of you. There comes a time when all of us need to be recognized for what we are. Everyone is clamouring for their fifteen minutes of fame: quick, before the Sun moves on to modest Virgo, let's put ourselves on view, where the celestial orb shines brightest. If our destiny is written in the stars, let's make sure we put the signs where all can see. This card suggests remaking old contacts and looking for new ones, reinventing ourselves with a fresh presentation. As the old movie stars said, any publicity is better than no publicity!

IN A READING

Applying for a job by presenting your CV and other information about yourself.
Being introduced to someone who attracts you or is helpful to you.
Pushing yourself forward for an important job.
A little harmless boasting about your achievements.
Giving yourself a more daring and different exterior in order to get noticed.

WHEN REVERSED

Finding that someone is spreading adverse stories about you.
Failing to get the recognition you feel you deserve.
A creative project that fails, through bad or inadequate presentation.
Spreading your abilities too thinly to have any real effect.

LUGHNASADH

CARD 4

Season AUTUMN

Keyword NOURISHMENT

Element EARTH

Month AUGUST

Week 4TH

Astrology VIRGO / CANCER

THE IMAGE: *An angel carrying the disc of the Sun flies above a young woman. From the disc, five rays of pure creative power emanate towards the woman. She looks up with raised hands to receive the Sun's energy. An image of a bird, symbolizing the spiritual life, soars towards the Sun.*

In the fourth week of August the Sun starts its journey through the earth sign Virgo. As a number four card it has the influence of the caring sign Cancer. This is both a physically and emotionally nourishing combination, relating to the well-being and health of the querent. It signifies a period when following a sensible health regime is of great importance, as is a working environment that is well ordered and functioning perfectly. The smooth running of a project requires much concentration and patience. Every aspect of our life should be rewarding and enriching, in order that we may enjoy our day-to-day experiences. This is a time to make sure all we do contributes to the maintenance of our inner and outer health, and to establish a balance between work and family life. Virgo is a perfectionist and can become distraught when system and order are disrupted. The desire to achieve the perfect balance can lead to excessive analysis and criticism, which will defeat the object.

IN A READING

Starting an alternative health regime. Looking after someone who is ill.
Studying health issues or working for a health organization.
Introducing a new work system to increase efficiency.
Doing background research for an organization.
Learning about new business techniques.

WHEN REVERSED

Being starved of creative imagination or stimulation.
Reaching a period where life seems depressingly dull and uneventful.
Having support that you need, withdrawn. A family loss or dispute.
Being let down or deserted by a partner who you relied on.

LUGHNASADH

CARD 5

Season AUTUMN
Keyword MANAGEMENT
Element EARTH
Month SEPTEMBER
Week 1ST
Astrology VIRGO/LEO

THE IMAGE: *A capable and direct woman holds above her head, amid growing plants, a male and a female figure. They are under her direction and rely on her to guide them in their work. The woman is strict but just in managing those who work for her and in fulfilling her responsibilities to the work in hand.*

The Sun is in Virgo during the first week of September, bringing a well-organized and self-critical feeling to this card. It is ruled by the boss sign Leo, and this combination creates a working arrangement. Leo's position in any situation is one of leadership, while Virgo's is as the perfect personal assistant. This is an ideal partnership, for Virgo's modest attitude is to do the background work for Leo's impressive and showy front. The card symbolizes essential back-up work that is undertaken in a quietly efficient way, to ensure the success of any project. Each role in the management team is indispensable and each values the other. This card often appears when employment or health questions are asked. It may even suggest a pairing of the two issues, as in working for a health organization. This is a period when super-critical attention must be paid to the work in question. In the agricultural year, this card represents the forming and organizing of teams of workers for gathering in the harvest. It is a time when order and regulation are of utmost importance to the quick and efficient management and despatch of the fruits to market.

IN A READING

Promotion to a position of responsibility within an organization.
Recognition of services to an organization.
Living carefully on a small budget.
A new responsibility that is suddenly imposed on you.
Entering into a profitable new partnership.
An offer from someone important and influential.

WHEN REVERSED

Feeling that your life is in a mess. Having no effective system.
Energy wasted on badly planned projects.
Jumping into something without first considering the methods or the outcome.

LUGHNASADH

CARD 6

Season AUTUMN
Keyword DETAIL
Element EARTH
Month SEPTEMBER
Week 2ND
Astrology VIRGO / VIRGO

THE IMAGE: *A highly decorative embroidery picture shows a flower basket with many different plants and leaves as the motif. It is meticulous work and four tiny earth sprites arrange and position the delicate and detailed work perfectly.*

Virgo rules the number six cards, and as this card falls in the second week of September it is also Sun-ruled by Virgo, giving a double influence of this sign. Traditionally, Virgo represents a nurturing Mother Earth and the enjoyment of the fruits of careful husbandry. This indicates gains through hard and conscientious labour. The perfection that contributed to a successful harvest must now be continued in the orderly preservation of nature's bounty. Achievements mustn't be wasted, but should be stored carefully until needed. Being an earth card it will refer more to tangible and physical situations than emotional, mental or creative matters, though not to their exclusion. When these latter qualities are expressed, it will often be in terms of physical actions – a gift, cash assistance or working on behalf of someone else, for example. This card also represents health, both of the querent and those around them. It denotes discipline with regard to diet and a firm resolution to stick to a good physical regime for the benefit of our wellbeing. It represents modest workers who remain in the background, or civil servants who build the steady foundations on which the more flamboyant state their case. It also signifies those involved in alternative medicine or the practical running of health clinics.

IN A READING

Reaping the benefits of a great deal of detailed work.
An award for an achievement. Passing an exam.
Acquiring the necessary finance to enable investment in a sound future project.
Good health based on sensible living.

WHEN REVERSED

Discovering a proposition is not as it seemed. Failing to read the small print.
Finding out that you aren't entitled to something you thought was yours.
A contract or work proposal that is not in your favour.

LUGHNASADH

CARD 7

Season AUTUMN
Keyword FRIENDSHIP
Element EARTH
Month SEPTEMBER
Week 3RD
Astrology VIRGO / LIBRA

THE IMAGE: *Two young girls clasp hands to greet each other. One holds a flower as a gift and a symbol of their close companionship. Their responses display the feminine side of our nature, and the youth of the two friends represents the continuing vitality of the relationship.*

The third week in September sees the Sun move through the last degrees of the earth sign Virgo. Libra rules the seventh card and so partnerships, teamwork and even marriage are on the agenda. This combination indicates much close and intimate discussion, with great understanding of each other's point of view. It can signify legal questions and issues concerning rights and justice. The Libran is a born diplomat who can easily see the value of both sides of any question. This, coupled with Virgo's sharp and analytical mind, is a recipe for solving legal matters. Virgo's ruling planet is the sharp-witted Mercury, and this adds to the card a flair for good conversation and general communication. This duo are typical of close friends who can chatter to each other for hours on end about almost any subject under the Sun. If the relationship in question is a marriage or close partnership, it is based more on friendship than sex. Whatever form the partnership takes, this card shows that it is destined to be long term.

IN A READING

An important discussion with an old friend.
Renewing an old friendship after a few years apart.
A close relationship based on good conversation or a mutual interest.
Finding new friends within a club or leisure interest.
Marriage counselling or taking a position advising people with problems.
Taking advice yourself.

WHEN REVERSED

Emotional distress after losing a friend or the break-up of a partnership.
An inability to make a close and sustaining friendship.
Being unable to give yourself wholeheartedly
to a relationship for fear of rejection.
Feeling helpless through being unable to help a friend in difficulty.

LUGHNASADH

CARD 8

Season AUTUMN

Keyword INTENSITY

Element EARTH

Month SEPTEMBER

Week 4TH

Astrology LIBRA / SCORPIO

THE IMAGE: *A sky dragon creates a storm with gales and lightning that flashes across an oppressively dark and ominous sky. A strong, young tree is still able to bend in the onslaught and is ready to spring back when the storm has subsided.*

In the fourth week of September the Sun passes from Virgo into Libra. Card eight has the natural ruler Scorpio. Relationships and teamwork are the Libran specialities, and passion and intensity are the Scorpion's strong points, making for an interesting but possibly stormy time. Libra's ability to see both sides of any question makes this character a natural socializer. The Scorpio side of the partnership, however, is more dogmatic, and passionately takes one side or the other. In fact this Mars-ruled sign is more likely to feel comfortable with an extreme view than one that is more neutral. Libra is about balance, so the middle is a more comfortable place than being perched on the edge. So, when this card appears, there will be long and intense discussions leading to heated arguments. It is likely to end with one party taking the easy way out and making a compromise. Although this combination of air and water can engender a stormy debate, this will be a necessary culmination of a situation that has reached a serious state of indecision. The air will be cleared and there will be a calm atmosphere in which to move forward.

IN A READING

A need to resolve a dispute and clear the air.
A heated argument that forces you to back down.
A disagreement in which a third party must adjudicate.
Taking legal action over an issue.
A break-up of a friendship through unreasonable behaviour.
Setting the pattern for a new attitude to a relationship.

WHEN REVERSED

Being able to ride a stormy quarrel with friends and make peace.
Deciding to forgive a personal attack on yourself and get on with your life.
Being strong enough not to take offence easily.
Relief at deciding against taking legal action.

9 LUGHNASADH

OCTOBER 1ST WEEK
PILGRIMAGE

LUGHNASADH
CARD 9

Season AUTUMN
Keyword PILGRIMAGE
Element EARTH
Month OCTOBER
Week 1ST
Astrology LIBRA / SAGITTARIUS

THE IMAGE: *In front of a blue sky a horse with two riders – one male and one female – canters friskily. The man carries a torch of enlightenment and wisdom. The pair are on a pilgrimage and friends travel on their Sagittarian mounts towards their goal. It is a quest for knowledge.*

In the first week of October the Sun is moving through the sign of Libra. The ruler of the nine card is Sagittarius. The sociable Libran needs people and the adventure-seeking Sagittarian craves travel. The combination produces the keyword 'pilgrimage'. The Archer's basic drive is to travel both mentally and physically, needing to continuously acquire knowledge and experience through constant movement. Other people and other places are a necessary part of this sign's life adventure. Libra craves companionship and conversation, and in this card combination they won't mind how far they travel to get it. It is a happy card that describes those who have similar interests and are willing to go to great lengths to further them. It is as if life is one great pilgrimage to the holy shrines of their passions. The card is a strong indicator of some kind of teamwork or enterprise, and it may suggest the joining of a group with a particular philosophy or objective.

IN A READING

A holiday with a group of like-minded people.
Being attracted to a new, or alternative, philosophy.
Working for a travel organization. Moving abroad for a time.
Taking a further education course. Learning another language.
An important contact with a friend or acquaintance abroad.

WHEN REVERSED

Being carried along with a group or organization
with which you no longer have any affinity.
Leaving a cult or religion because it was leading you in the wrong direction.
Being let down by someone from abroad.

10 LUGHNASADH △

OCTOBER 2ND WEEK
CONFORMITY

LUGHNASADH

CARD 10

Season AUTUMN
Keyword CONFORMITY
Element EARTH
Month OCTOBER
Week 2ND
Astrology LIBRA / CAPRICORN

THE IMAGE: *A decorated vase holds a symmetrical flower arrangement. The shape of the vase follows the profiles of two faces that mirror each other. As we concentrate on the faces, the vase moves into the background of the picture.*

All number ten cards are ruled by the ambitious, but orderly, sign Capricorn. In the second week of October the Sun still moves through Libra. Capricorn's desire is to see things working efficiently in a predictable and organized manner, and more often than not the Goat would prefer to be the one doing the organizing. Libra likes harmony and the pleasure of good sociable relationships. This combination keeps the wheels of society well oiled and running smoothly. A belief in a good working system demands that all conform to the traditions and laws that are set up for this purpose, and this system is essential for any large body of people to live together harmoniously. This sounds reasonable but in some cases the conformity is taken to extremes. With this card there can be an exceptional version of this theme, where someone lives by what others think to the exclusion of their own feelings and individuality. It is possible to be an individualist and act on our own volition without disturbing the way society is run. We may even question the rules and attempt to change them if they are outdated or unfair.

IN A READING

Being afraid to be seen doing something different from the rest.
Being reprimanded for stepping out of line.
Feeling jealous of someone else's position.
Doing what is expected of you in order to achieve your desires.
Taking a responsible position within your circle or community.
Keeping up with those around you in material possessions.

WHEN REVERSED

Having the courage to go your own way and be truthful to your beliefs.
Feeling secure in not caring what the world thinks of you.
Making a conscious decision to be different in some way
without being antisocial.

11 LUGHNASADH

OCTOBER 3RD WEEK
FREEDOM

LUGHNASADH

CARD 11

Season AUTUMN

Keyword FREEDOM

Element EARTH

Month OCTOBER

Week 3RD

Astrology LIBRA / AQUARIUS

THE IMAGE: *A wild-haired figure sits astride a strange birdfish in swooping flight. In its beak the birdfish carries a branch with berries that contain the seeds of invention. The eccentric creature is a symbol of the complexity of Aquarius which, although it is called the Water Carrier, is in fact an air sign.*

The eleventh card brings with it the rebellious sign Aquarius. This combines with the Sun still moving through Libra this week. We have two compatible air signs which produce a card that is about easy and frequent communication. Aquarius and Libra can discuss new thoughts and brilliant ideas endlessly, creating an atmosphere where situations can be explored freely with open minds. Some of the conservative ways of the previous card 'Conformity' will be tossed around and rejected, but not without intelligent analysis to find improved replacements. Aquarius has a particular ability to think laterally – to take an idea and stand it on end just to see if it works better that way. They are the zodiac's inventors, and even the most ordinary of subjects shows a spark of this enviable talent when Aquarius is involved. Libra is the best sign to bounce ideas off, giving an immediate response and acting as a switch that displays the other side of the coin. This is a great card for those who wish to break loose from a long spell in a well-worn rut.

IN A READING

Running a campaign to change something well established.
Breaking away from an old routine and starting something new.
Questioning someone's authority.
An ideas session with regard to a failing business.
Going into partnership with someone to make a living out of giving advice.
Feeling free after leaving an unbearable situation.

WHEN REVERSED

Longing to escape from a predictable and monotonous routine.
Sitting back and waiting to be rescued from your own lethargy.
Living vicariously through a more eccentric friend's exploits. Feeling trapped.

| 12 | LUGHNASADH | △ |

m,ℋ | OCTOBER 4TH WEEK
EXTREME CRAZE |

LUGHNASADH

CARD 12

Season AUTUMN
Keyword EXTREME CRAZE
Element EARTH
Month OCTOBER
Week 4TH
Astrology SCORPIO / PISCES

THE IMAGE: *A salmonlike fish leaps angrily past a dark cloud to the stars. It is passionate in its objective and follows its path single-mindedly. It represents the idealism and fantasy of Pisces imbued with the passion and extreme nature of the Scorpion.*

The last card of autumn, number twelve, is ruled by the imaginative and idealistic sign Pisces. In the fourth week of October the Sun moves into Scorpio. Two water signs have a rapport that is almost psychic. Scorpio does nothing by halves and will go to extremes to explore the limits of the shared sense world. Pisces has a chameleon-like quality that allows it to be whatever its partner chooses. (This reflects the Greek myth in which sailors were lured to their doom by sirens who appeared before them as a beautiful version of whatever their victim desired.) This combination, for whatever the outcome, is involved with transformation, persuasion and even deception. Harmonious as these two signs are, there is something unreal here. If the issue concerned has to do with fantasy in the form of creative expression, then this card could suggest that it is the kind of thing that would tap into the feelings of the masses and become a craze. On a personal level it can be blindly passionate, obsessive and a complete delusion to the detriment of the person, or persons, involved.

IN A READING

Following a cult, whether religious or otherwise.
Going to extreme ends to pursue an idea.
Becoming involved with a craze or a hugely popular person.
Involvement with an idea that catches the imagination of the public.
Involvement with the fashion or pop industry.
Having a good understanding of public taste and being able to exploit it.

WHEN REVERSED

Living a complete illusion. Having a role model revealed as unworthy.
Discovering you have been deceived for a long time by someone you look up to.
An interest or obsession that is taking over your life.
A self-destructive habit or passion that is impossible to deny.

WINTER SOLSTICE

*Sun in Capricorn on
or around 22 December*

On this day the Sun enters the patient and organized earth sign of Capricorn. It is a period of conservation and organization. The fields are allowed to rest before next year's planting, tools are repaired and accounts are made up. It is a quiet time of no direct movement but plenty of work. The Winter Solstice is celebrated in cultures all over the world. This beginning of the solar year is a celebration of light and the rebirth of the Sun. In ancient Europe it was known as Yule, from the Norse, Jul, meaning wheel. The Christmas tradition of a decorated tree has its origins in the pagan Yule celebration. Families would bring a live tree into the home to protect the wood spirits from the cold during the bitter winter months. Small treats of food were hung from the branches for the spirits to eat, and a five-pointed star – the pentagram, a magical symbol of the five elements – was placed at the very top of the tree. The reindeer, another Yule-related image, resembles the Horned God – the Green Man. Mistletoe, sacred because it mysteriously grew on the most sacred tree, the oak, was cut down and a branch given to each family to be hung in their doorway as a symbol of good luck. The Winter Solstice marks a key part of the year's natural cycle. In a material sense the Sun begins a new journey towards longer days and a period of new growth and renewal of the world once again. In a spiritual sense, it is a reminder that in order for any new path to begin, the old one must cease.

IN A READING

It is important to look at the general implication of the other cards close by, as they will be enhanced or influenced by this strong card. It will emphasize that no matter what the general sense of the interpretation is, there will be some time before the desired outcome is a reality. This card calls for patience. All will be rewarded in the end.

1	SAMHAIN	▽

| ♏︎♈︎ | NOVEMBER 1ST WEEK
STRENGTH | ❄ |

SAMHAIN

CARD 1

Season WINTER
Keyword STRENGTH
Element AIR
Month NOVEMBER
Week 1ST
Astrology SCORPIO / ARIES

THE IMAGE: *An invincible, aggressive Martian Sun-dragon – half beast, half scorpion – prepares for attack. The Aries half is the lamb that when challenged becomes a lion. The Scorpio half is ever ready to find an adversary's weakest point and strike with its deadly sting.*

The first week of November finds the Sun in the powerful water sign Scorpio, and as this is a number one card it is joined by Aries. Being the first zodiac sign, Aries is comfortable with the role of leader, and is to be found at the forefront of any situation. It is a heroic sign prepared to venture into anything, with the unknown holding little fear for the bold, brave Ram. The nature of the strategist-supreme

Scorpio is to try out extremes of all kinds to discover the limits; to understand each potential danger, the task is to find its weakest point and then go in with the scorpion's sting. The partnership we have here is Scorpio the army general and Aries the hero – a fighting combination that produces enormous strength. As in ancient communities where there was a threat from dangers that would destroy everyday life – storms that destroyed crops and property, or invaders that stole cattle and land – this card shows a need for rough courage, alertness and determination. All that is truly loved and worked for is worth defending, and great strength must be constantly maintained.

IN A READING

The need to stand up for your rights or possessions.
Feeling that you are under attack.
A troublesome situation that you are unable to walk away from.
Finding yourself involved in someone else's battle.
Having to take sides in a tricky situation.

WHEN REVERSED

Finding it impossible to accept your own anger and potential aggression.
Taking the coward's way out and turning tail.
Behaving in a way that pushes, or encourages, someone else
to act out your aggression.

SAMHAIN
CARD 2

Season WINTER
Keyword PREPAREDNESS
Element AIR
Month NOVEMBER
Week 2ND
Astrology SCORPIO / TAURUS

THE IMAGE: *A warrior with armour, a shield and a battle-axe sits astride a bull, demonstrating defiance. The bull is a symbol of solid and fearless defence that will only attack as a last resort. The Scorpio warrior is prepared to wait as long as necessary to discover potential threats and weaknesses in any situation.*

The Sun is moving through Scorpio in the second week of November and this combines with the number two sign Taurus. Both of these signs are concerned with the sensual world. Taurus is involved with personal possessions and sensations, whereas Scorpio is about shared sensation and finances. Although they are opposite signs in the zodiac circle, these two have a great deal in common where protectiveness and forward-thinking are involved. Each prepares itself for any eventuality and needs to know how it would react in the event of any unpleasant or disconcerting circumstance. Taurus makes sure that all is supported by firm foundations and good groundwork. Scorpio takes the trouble to find the weak spot in any potential hazard so that it may be defeated. All in all, this card demands care and preparedness against the possibility of upsets as far as possible. Taurus is prepared to defend and Scorpio to attack – a formidable team that is ready to throw itself into the business of keeping what it values. With this card the possession referred to is, more often than not, money.

IN A READING

Careful investment of your own or other people's money.
Taking out insurance. Taking precautions against theft or fraud.
Doing a credit search on someone you have important dealings with.
Assisting someone you are close to with their finances.
Putting some money aside for an emergency.

WHEN REVERSED

Going into a battle over property without sufficient preparation.
Acting naively in a negotiation and taking everything at face value.
A chance of losing valuable possessions or assets
through lack of care and forethought.
Giving up without a struggle through indifference or laziness.

SAMHAIN
CARD 3

Season WINTER
Keyword MIND POWER
Element AIR
Month NOVEMBER
Week 3RD
Astrology SCORPIO / GEMINI

THE IMAGE: *In a starry sky is a swirling, seven-coiled labyrinth representing the seven personal planets. Pale moonlight glows through its curving path. This is a symbol of thinking before acting, where the challenge is to the intellect and imagination. Below is a symmetrical pattern that shows twin birds chattering.*

During the third week of November the Sun moves through the last degrees of Scorpio. Gemini rules the number three card and here we have a combination that indicates acute and perceptive thinking. Gemini is the zodiac's information gatherer. Rarely specialists in any one subject, the Twins set about collecting just enough information to see the complete picture clearly, using as many sources as necessary.

Scorpio can take the given information and use it with powerful persuasion and great effect. Whatever the cause, the Scorpion is the zodiac's best propagandist and when these two signs unite there is a formidable force of mind power that can turn the heads and views of many. This card indicates the influence of someone articulate who will speak out about any subject. It may suggest the presence of a guru or perhaps a powerful and charismatic figure who becomes involved in the situation or is concerned with the querent. Sometimes this will reflect a period of clear and eloquent thinking on the part of the questioner, which gains support from prominent circles.

IN A READING

Being open to the persuasive influence of a leader or guru.
Being smooth-talked into something slightly out of character.
Having the right words to really persuade others to your point of view.
Having the verbal ability to clear the air after a tense and difficult impasse.
Regretting that you have been taken in by a clever salesperson.

WHEN REVERSED

Using an unfair argument. Lying to achieve selfish ends.
Deliberately using someone else's weakness to gain power over them.
Placing the blame for something that you have done on to someone else.
Malicious gossip. A fanatical mental obsession.

SAMHAIN

CARD 4

Season WINTER

Keywords TRAVEL, FAMILY

Element AIR

Month NOVEMBER

Week 4TH

Astrology SAGITTARIUS / CANCER

THE IMAGE: *A family in a small boat rides through a storm at sea. The father optimistically guides and reassures, and the mother holds a protective hand towards the children. They are united in their adventure and will be strengthened by their shared courage and fears. Their journey is life.*

During the fourth week of November the Sun moves from Scorpio into Sagittarius and the fourth winter card is ruled by the sign Cancer. This is an upheaval in the sense that Cancer is one of the most rooted of signs, inclined to build a secure and comfortable home with no desire to move far away from it. Sagittarius, however, is the eternal wanderer forever searching for greener fields in far distant places.

When these contrasting signs are combined, there is certainly conflict. The card indicates a necessity to move on, that something has occurred bringing about the need to move house and uproot the family and all that is dear. The reason may even be a marvellous opportunity for everyone but the resulting losses of the comfortable, familiar and everyday pleasures will not be passed up without a great deal of concern. The Sagittarian side will adore the opportunity to discover the exciting potential of the new home, but the Cancerian will look back with pain in their heart for that which is being left behind. This is a marriage of opposites, but it has great strength and can adapt, thus enriching the contrasting facets of each sign.

IN A READING

An opportunity abroad or in another part of the country.
Having to move house for financial reasons. A long family holiday.
A change of job. Working with someone from abroad.
Someone – possibly a relation – coming to stay with the family for a while.

WHEN REVERSED

A detached or separated family.
A stormy family dispute over property inheritances
or just a clash of personalities.
A family venture or business that is battling to keep going.
A family division caused by a conflict of cultures.

| 5 | SAMHAIN | ▽ |

DECEMBER 1ST WEEK
FESTIVAL

SAMHAIN

CARD 5

Season WINTER
Keyword FESTIVAL
Element AIR
Month DECEMBER
Week 1ST
Astrology SAGITTARIUS / LEO

THE IMAGE: *Three figures in grotesque – but amusing – fancy dress with animal and bird headdresses perform a well-known dance. They are celebrating an annual festival that has become a much-loved tradition over the centuries. Every year each actor in the small pageant dons their costume and plays their joyous part.*

The first week of December sees the Sun move through the sign of Sagittarius. This is a happy period and in many countries it is traditionally a time of celebration – in Holland the feast day of Sinterklaas is 6 December. The fifth card is ruled by the lavish, luxury-loving sign Leo, so here we have two compatible fire signs. Leo is showy and sociable – the perfect party giver – generous to a fault, for with the celestial Lion no expense is spared. Jupiter-ruled Sagittarius is the zodiac's fun sign. The Centaur will play and join in with any entertainment at the drop of a hat. This card represents the excitement that comes from approaching the end of a year and from beginning the annual celebrations that will continue throughout the month. In today's culture, this is demonstrated in the decoration of the shops and high streets in preparation for the seasonal gift giving that culminates at the end of December in most countries. When this card is dealt in a reading, it shows a feeling of immense goodwill and indicates a reason to celebrate and share our good fortune.

IN A READING

A period when you can sit back and appreciate the good things you have.
Being with a group of good-natured and fun-loving people.
Feeling the support of a traditionally secure and loving family.

WHEN REVERSED

Disappointment because a long-awaited celebration is cancelled.
Reaching the end of a period of very hard work,
only to find it was a waste of time.
Putting on a show that ends in failure or anticlimax.

6   SAMHAIN   ▽

x↗ ♍ | DECEMBER 2ND WEEK HEALTH, YOGA | ❄

SAMHAIN

CARD 6

Season WINTER

Keywords HEALTH, YOGA

Element AIR

Month DECEMBER

Week 2ND

Astrology SAGITTARIUS / VIRGO

THE IMAGE: *A meditating shaman or wizard – antlered and holding two flaming torches – sits relaxed in a ritual position on the ground. At his breast is the earth cross, and his knee touches the Sun disc. Stars and crystals decorate the luminous sky.*

Virgo rules this card, and as in this suit the card falls in the second week of December it is accompanied by the Sun moving through Sagittarius. The combination of the philosophical, far-travelling Archer and the Virginal health lover suggests a new health regime. Both signs can be attracted to the philosophies of distant lands, and what better than the strongly disciplined attention to the chakras and the yogic posture of Eastern culture? Virgo's desire to see everything working efficiently stretches from well-organized work patterns to a regular and healthy routine to cater for all our bodily needs. Sagittarian drive follows the current philosophy as far as it goes, seeking to constantly improve their knowledge of the world. The two signs working together could suggest a business venture in alternative health, focusing on areas such as yoga and acupuncture. If this isn't the case, there is certainly much to be gained from paying attention to health and fitness.

IN A READING

A desire to go on a strict health and fitness plan. Taking up a sport.
A trip abroad that leads you to become captivated
by the ways of another culture.
Trying out, or having tuition in, alternative health therapies.
Simplifying your life and desires and getting closer to nature.

WHEN REVERSED

Seeking an easy way to escape problems through the use
of alcohol, pills or other intoxicants.
Being addicted to something and needing help to go 'cold turkey'.
Having no respect for yourself.
Reaching a stage where your health is affected
by your harmful and disordered lifestyle.
Finding that bad organization is causing life and work to become a real struggle.

SAMHAIN

CARD 7

Season WINTER

Keyword REUNION

Element AIR

Month DECEMBER

Week 3RD

Astrology SAGITTARIUS / LIBRA

THE IMAGE: *A man and a woman greet each other with a friendly embrace. Their clothes are elaborately decorated and embroidered, symbolizing the rich experiences they have gathered since last they met. Their lives have separated for a while as each was busy with their own concerns. They have plenty to catch up on.*

In the third week of December the Sun passes through the last seven degrees of Sagittarius. It joins here with the ruler of the seventh card Libra, and indicates the meeting of old friends. People from abroad and contacts with foreign countries are denoted by this card. The Libran lover of good company keeps in contact with a vast number of friends and acquaintances, and at this time of the year makes special contacts. It is a time for reunion, for the resolving of old quarrels and catching up on news from long-parted friends. This is a time when we put aside thoughts of our busy year to think of others. Jupiter, the ruler of Sagittarius, is the planet of expansion and growth. It symbolizes not only a reunion with missed friends, but also with our own childhood and youth: a reminder, through the many children we see at seasonal family gatherings, of our own growing up. It is a reunion with our past. This card can also represent an interest in genealogy and the vital links with our genetic heritage. When it appears in a reading, it can indicate an unexpected reunion with someone we have forgotten.

IN A READING

A school or work reunion. The sudden reappearance of an old friend. Rediscovering a talent or ability that you hadn't used for years. Rediscovering your real self through a change of circumstances. An important family gathering.

WHEN REVERSED

A past traumatic love affair that comes back to haunt you. A skeleton that comes out of the closet. Disappointment at meeting an old friend and finding that you no longer have anything in common. Losing contact with an old and valued friend.

8   SAMHAIN   ▽

♑♏ | DECEMBER 4TH WEEK TRADITION, RITUAL | ❄

SAMHAIN

CARD 8

Season WINTER
Keywords TRADITION, RITUAL
Element AIR
Month DECEMBER
Week 4TH
Astrology CAPRICORN / SCORPIO

THE IMAGE: *This is a powerful image of an attractive, dignified and charismatic man. His hair is a flaming halo, giving the godlike quality of the creative Sun. Two ribbons twine around the halo and become this season's plant – the magical mistletoe. This figure is authority and is to be obeyed and respected.*

The Sun moves into Capricorn in the fourth week of December and, as the eighth winter card, it is accompanied by the sign Scorpio. A stickler for tradition and the way things have always been run, the Sea-goat loves to organize and see that things are done appropriately. Scorpio shares much of its fellow water sign, Cancer's, love of the past and history and, in this combination, becomes a willing partner. Traditions and rituals give us a focal point with which to punctuate the humdrum of everyday life. Our regular times of celebration and occasions for ceremony – whether they are religious or secular – are essential markers for the seasons. It is important that, through these rituals, we maintain a link with our past and a close contact with the simpler and more earth-aware part of our history. As an essentially social animal there is a human need – no matter how much we feel we need to express our individuality – to occasionally all be doing the same thing at the same time; to feel at one with everyone else.

IN A READING

Feeling a need to conform.
Going along with a ritual in order to be sociable rather than
because you believe in what you are doing.
Setting up a regular event among friends or those with a similar interest.
Being elected as a member of a club that has very strict rules and regulations.
An interest in the philosophy of occult or magical matters.

WHEN REVERSED

Not wishing to conform, standing alone as an outsider.
Being left out on the fringe of a group or organization.
Taking conformity to the extreme.
Sticking rigidly to the rules even though they aren't appropriate in this situation.

9   SAMHAIN

JANUARY 1ST WEEK
RELIGION, BELIEF

SAMHAIN

CARD 9

Season WINTER

Keywords RELIGION, BELIEF

Element AIR

Month JANUARY

Week 1ST

Astrology CAPRICORN / SAGITTARIUS

THE IMAGE: *A shaman, priest or wizard stands by the symbols of his beliefs – the temple, the holy oils and the words of the enlightened ones. His hand is raised in a divine blessing and, as our connection with the gods, he convinces us of his truths.*

Sagittarius is the sign ruling all nine cards and in the first week of January it is in combination with the Sun in Capricorn. Sagittarius, in its far-seeking quest for a life philosophy, finds a serious partner in the orderly and convention-keeping Capricorn. This card, when it appears in a reading, represents our beliefs. This may or may not be a religion, but it is what we feel to be the ultimate truth and what we need to believe in to be comfortable with the way we choose to live. We tend to use belief as a support when we encounter a problem or when we are afraid. This is a throwback to our past when knowledge was in its infancy. Our ancestors believed in gods whose anger, expressed in thunder and lightning, was appeasable and whose assistance in making the earth fertile was to be bought with prayers, sacrifices and gifts. Many today still believe in buying and selling favours with their deities. This is a small part of the meaning of this card. What is more important here is the personal morality that results from our experience and gathered knowledge.

IN A READING

Expounding your philosophy.
Finding a philosophy or religion that appeals to you.
Rejecting the religion you were brought up with
in favour of your own philosophy.
Seeking help with a difficult moral problem.
Attraction to an Eastern philosophy or religion of another country.

WHEN REVERSED

Having your earlier beliefs weakened by your own confidence and reasoning.
A need to question the things you have accepted unthinkingly since childhood.
Suffering persecution for your beliefs or non-belief.
An extreme or fundamental attitude to a set of beliefs.

SAMHAIN

CARD 10

Season WINTER
Keywords LAW, RULES
Element AIR
Month JANUARY
Week 2ND
Astrology CAPRICORN / CAPRICORN

THE IMAGE: *A monarch seated on a throne holds a sword and a book of law. Around him are courtiers and armed soldiers – the support and the power to enforce law and order. Three figures await judgement on the cases they have brought to the royal court.*

In the second week of January the Sun is moving through Capricorn. The number ten card is also ruled by this sign so we have a double Capricorn emphasis. The focus is on law and order; to run a farm, village, town or country we must have laws and we also need people to see that they are adhered to. This is the very essence of the talents of the organizing sign Capricorn. Laws are created to protect the majority, so they are never absolutely perfect. They aren't necessarily about justice; they are a way to keep everything running smoothly and preventing chaos or anarchy. This card suggests that the law should be studied and exploited if you wish it to work for you. Conversely, it is a warning that you may be involved with someone who is breaking (or bending) the law. And in order to succeed at any game we must play by the rules so here, again, we are urged to abide by the law or whatever is usual for the situation under discussion.

IN A READING

Having to take legal advice to put something right.
Adapting to someone else's set of rules in order to get what you want.
Seeking to put right an injustice. Being the victim of an unfair decision.
Taking on a position of authority with a small group or community.

WHEN REVERSED

Being on the wrong side of the law. Regretting committing an illegal act.
Being punished by events, for a past weakness.
Finding that someone for whom you have made life difficult
is now in a position of power over you.

| 11 | SAMHAIN | ▽ |

JANUARY 3RD WEEK
REBELLION

SAMHAIN
CARD 11

Season WINTER
Keyword REBELLION
Element AIR
Month JANUARY
Week 3RD
Astrology CAPRICORN / AQUARIUS

THE IMAGE: *A grand statue of a king in full regal costume has lost its crown; a dark cloud and a sharp flash of lightning – symbolizing rebellion – have severed its head. The people cheer as the despotic ruler is deposed.*

In the third week of January the Sun is passing through the last few degrees of Capricorn, and is partnered by the eleventh sign Aquarius. Winter is the time to prepare for the next year, and as spring approaches new thinking begins to enter the agenda. Was last year a success? Do the same methods apply now? Aquarius questions every-thing and accepts nothing at face value. Just because things have always been done a certain way doesn't necessarily mean they are the best now. The Water Carrier is the rebel of the zodiac and Capricorn is the traditionalist. Aquarius's rebellion, however, is not without a keen sense of right and wrong; change and movement are necessary to prevent stagnation, and challenge is the means by which we update redundant ways. So in this card we see conflict and an indication that something must be questioned in order to bring about new and better conditions in which to operate successfully. There is an awareness that the quiet restfulness of the winter is about to be awakened by the call of spring.

IN A READING

Joining a group devoted to change of some kind.
Putting your name to a good cause.
Questioning an old system that no longer applies.
Requiring people around you to see you in a different light.
Setting up conditions for a new and better working relationship with someone.
A drastic change of routine to improve life in some way.

WHEN REVERSED

A plan to oust somebody bounces back on you.
Becoming the scapegoat for a failed attempt at changing conditions.
Being treated as a rebel and not taken seriously.
Attempting a violent overthrow or shock on someone who oppresses you.
Being in trouble for antisocial behaviour.

SAMHAIN

CARD 12

Season WINTER
Keyword TEMPTATION
Element AIR
Month JANUARY
Week 4TH
Astrology AQUARIUS / PISCES

THE IMAGE: *Two beautifully dressed angels stand either side of a tree. In the sky are the Moon and the Sun – the feminine and the masculine luminaries. Entwined around the tree and nuzzling the woman's hand is a serpent. This is a fully dressed, worldly Adam and Eve, as opposed to the original pair, unclothed and innocent.*

In the fourth week of January the Sun moves into the inventive sign of Aquarius. Number twelve cards are ruled by the intuitive Pisces, which adds a creative, mind-stretching quality to this card. Here, all the possibilities of fantasy and experimentation are explored uninhibitedly and with great abandon. Nothing is too outrageous or avant-garde. These two signs represent a mutual temptation, each bringing out the extreme possibilities of the other. It is as if the end of the cold winter is here and anything goes! It may not be a physical temptation and even if it is all in the mind it is no less exciting and stimulating. The planet that rules Aquarius is oddball, eccentric Uranus, while dreamy, sensitive Neptune rules Pisces. The chemistry here is seductive and pleasure bound. Both Aquarius and Pisces are humanitarian and caring with regard to those around them, and will rarely harm any but themselves through their self-delusion.

IN A READING

Giving in to a temptation. Being smooth-talked into accepting a proposition.
Bringing about a real outcome to something that was previously a fantasy.
Doing something that you know those close to you will disapprove of.
Being made an offer you can't refuse. Risking something illegal.
Living under an illusion.

WHEN REVERSED

Making a sacrifice for someone else's well-being.
Resisting temptation and feeling good about it.
Being offered an exploitive get-rich-quick plan and rejecting it.
Working to help those who have been led astray
by drugs, gambling or other temptations.
Helping others through knowledge of your own weaknesses.

THE LAYOUTS

Before you start reading the cards, take time to get to know the meanings we give for the runes and the four suits; the images are easy to remember and the keywords provide a gentle reminder. The interpretations given here are to feed your imagination. As with all divination tools the secret is to gradually develop your own feelings about the images and work with whatever speaks to you. Divination is an intensely personal thing and we can never develop a true perception by rote, simply obeying a strict set of rules as if the tarot was a card game. With regard to the spreads, the cards can be read in many ways and there is much written about tarot spreads of all kinds. This deck will work with all the traditional layouts and we include some specific ones here.

The Rune Cards in a Reading

The twenty-four major rune cards relate directly to the questioner. When they occur in a reading they will draw attention to some facet of the personality that is claiming recognition at the time. The characters we describe in the rune card interpretations will be reflected in our own psyche. Over and above the everyday questions that we ask of the tarot, the runic images present us with deeper questions that must be heeded. Each rune card has a powerful resonance within our inner understanding, and will give a deeper insight into what really lies beneath a seemingly simple enquiry. The runes surprise us, lecture us, lead us and point us to the path of self-revelation.

The Minor Arcana in a Reading

The minor cards refer less to the personality and more specifically to the events and possibilities in the life of the querent. When they appear, we must look for outside events that could influence the outcome. Each minor card has a meaning derived from the cycle of the Earth's seasons.

Imbolc, or spring, cards refer symbolically to the beginning of young life, and will reflect this in a reading. They show the start of situations and how they will maintain their growth or, indeed, fall by the wayside. Spring is an action time but, in the hustle and bustle of events, will only show the potential and not the conclusion of a situation.

Beltane, or summer, cards show the year's flowering stage. Just as young animal life establishes itself and plants give us the pleasure of their blossoms, so the questions we ask resolve themselves with bright and optimistic outcomes. Summer puts the best on show and the May, June and July cards give strong and definite answers.

Lughnasadh, or autumn, cards represent the harvest. After the blossoms the plants bear their fruits. These cards are reflected in a reading as the tangible benefits of the outcome of a question. This is the climax of the yearly cycle. The precious bounty is here to be enjoyed, and it will also become the seeds and roots for the future. August, September and October cards usually denote happy events and positive answers.

Samhain, or winter, cards reveal a period when those things that have had their time die off to be replaced in the next cycle. It is a time to rest and wait. In a reading, winter cards will always signify stagnation, an impasse or a need to sit back and let things take their course. Although this is a season for little movement, it doesn't necessarily imply hibernation for there is much to be done in preparation for the coming year.

THE CELTIC TREE LAYOUT

L ay out the cards in the sequence shown here, building the pattern to the final card. The trunk of the tree denotes the question and the factors that are for and against the successful outcome. The three cards spreading to the left show the development and causes in sequence from the distant past to the most recent. The top card at position 7 shows the outcome, and the three cards spreading to the right indicate where this outcome will lead in the future.

Lauren's Celtic Tree Reading

Lauren has taken her final exams and has acquired all the qualifications she needs to go to university, but she is in a dilemma. Two of her closest friends are planning to take a two-year sabbatical, backpacking around the world. Lauren is hungry for education, but also for adventure, and so the call of each of the alternatives is equally appealing. What should she do? We made the following reading.

POSITION 1 *The Question*
Samhain 7 *Reunion*

All number seven cards have the nature of Libra and as this one is placed in the third week of December when the Sun is in Sagittarius, we have a Libra–Sagittarius combination. This describes the question perfectly. Libra (the balance) always sees the value of both sides of a problem. This ensures a fair and considered answer, but makes for a great deal of indecision. Sagittarius rules both further education and

THE OUTCOME

THE PAST

THE FUTURE

7

Samhain 5

6

Samhain 12

8

Beltane 12

5

Rune 4 Os

9

Imbolc 2

4

Beltane 9

3 NEGATIVE INFLUENCE

Lughnasadh 1

10

Imbolc 6

2 POSITIVE INFLUENCE

Rune 3 Thorn

1 THE QUESTION

Samhain 7

long-distance travel. The idea of the card 'reunion' is developed here in two ways. If Lauren goes with her friends, it becomes a new way of enriching their friendship outside the simple day-to-day contacts at school, a strengthening of the link. If Lauren stays on and goes to university, she will not lose the contact, and both sides will have much to add to the reunion when the other girls arrive home. This card describes Lauren's current uncertainty very well. Samhain cards relate to air intellect and the question is, which of the alternatives would be of the greatest benefit to Lauren's mind? The month of December is seasonally a time of rest and indicates a waiting time before making the next move.

POSITION 2 *Positive Influence*
Rune 3 Thorn *Attack or defence*

To get a major rune card in this position bodes well for a good answer and also underlines the importance of the question. Thorn signifies attack or defence. As with the sharp thorn of the delicate rose, something beautifully precious is combined with a powerful protection. This defines again the dual nature of the question but signifies that Lauren will be well safeguarded whatever the final decision.

POSITION 3 *Negative Influence*
Lughnasadh 1 *Risk, gamble*

Here, two fire signs, Leo and Aries, combine to throw the lamb to the lion. The keyword 'risk' is encapsulated in this combination. Leo is always liable to take the fun option and is tempted by the big idea, and

Aries is the zodiac's most spontaneous sign. We must reserve our opinion for the time being, as the fact that there is a dilemma means the immediate response that Aries can't resist making would be unwise.

Positions 4, 5 and 6 are read as a trio and show the Past, or background, of the question.

POSITION 4 Beltane 9 *Celebration*
POSITION 5 Rune 4 Os *God, Odin, language*
POSITION 6 Samhain 12 *Temptation*

Card 4 (Beltane 9) is ruled by Sagittarius and Cancer and describes the family celebration over Lauren's scholarly achievements. Her hard work has been rewarded, and the rune Os in position 5 shows communication in the form of a revealing message or insight – the long-awaited results! In position 6, the winter card Samhain 12 is the nagging one. This card, suggesting temptation and ruled by impressionable Pisces and oddball Aquarius, sets the dream going. Fantasies of distant lands vie with intellectual brilliance at university – each equally attractive. What is the answer?

POSITION 7 *The Outcome*
Samhain 5 *Festival*

The sign combination of this card is Leo–Sagittarius and it is in December, the winter month of rest. Winter denotes a period of gentle preparation for the future and indicates that Lauren should take a break from the concentration of her intellectual studies and choose the backpacking option. This will be an exciting new adventure for her and will contribute to her continued education in a more relaxed manner than the last concentrated hard-working years.

The 'In a reading' section of the Samhain 5 card says: Being in the company of a group of good-natured and fun-loving people. Feeling the support of a traditionally secure and loving family.

Positions 8, 9 and 10 are read as a trio and show the Future as potential for the questioner.

POSITION 8 Beltane 12 *Vision*
POSITION 9 Imbolc 2 *Awakening*
POSITION 10 Imbolc 6 *Cleansing*

In position 8 we find summer card Beltane 12, in the water element and ruled by Pisces and Leo. Both these signs have a potential for great creative imagination and vision. This suggests that after her travels Lauren will, with that extra experience, be able to see her future quite differently and will work solidly towards her aims. In position 9, Imbolc 2 suggests the previously secure and cautious nature of Taurus is aroused by the originality of Aquarius, and tempted into new ideas with regard to the future. The indication is that, on her return, Lauren may not feel the need to go to university but will have developed new talents for her future. Finally, in position 10 another spring card, Imbolc 6, gives the combination of Virgo and Pisces and indicates a perfect future. Virgo is orderly and perfectionist and is concerned with health and work. Pisces is caring and sensitive to the needs of others. It is probable that Lauren's experience during her travels will have equipped her for a new occupation working with people in some caring way and maybe somewhere abroad.

The technique of reading is to see the images and keywords first as words, then to put these together as sentences, gradually developing the reading into a clear and viable story. So we have:

QUESTION: *reunion; attack or defence; risk, gamble*
PAST: *celebration; language; temptation*
OUTCOME: *festival*
FUTURE: *vision; awakening; cleansing*

THE SEASONS LAYOUT

For quick or daily practice readings, deal four cards in the form of a simple cross as shown, taking the seasons' positions as they are shown on the Sun's zodiac wheel (*see page 10*).

2 SUMMER

1 SPRING

3 AUTUMN

4 WINTER

SPRING *Card 1 will show the question's starting point.*
SUMMER *Card 2 represents flowering or possibilities.*
AUTUMN *Card 3 sees the appearance of fruits – the outcome.*
WINTER *Card 4 indicates the benefits gained.*

Edward's Seasons Reading

Edward is looking for a new apartment. He feels strongly about living in town but has been told by a friend about a great flat in a small converted stately home about thirty miles out of town. This is not on his agenda at all but the price is good, the flat spacious and in town he would only get a meagre two-roomed pad. Should he go to see the property? This is how the cards fell.

THE SPRING CARD Lughnasadh 3 *Publicity*

Being introduced to someone who attracts you or is helpful to you. Pushing yourself forward for an important job.

THE SUMMER CARD Lughnasadh 11 *Freedom*

Breaking away from an old routine and starting something new.

THE AUTUMN CARD Rune 18 Birca *Rebirth, awakening*

An exciting time for fresh beginnings and new adventures. Spiritual renewal. The acceptance of new ideas. Making a decision to change your life.

THE WINTER CARD **Beltane 4** *Tradition*

Taking on work involving history, perhaps relating to archaeology, antiques or museums. Links with distant relatives.

OUR INTERPRETATION The spring card (Lughnasadh 3) clearly refers to the friend who is raving about the flat and doing a good enough publicity job to at least get old stick-in-the-mud Edward interested in something a little different! Thinking that he has to be tied to the big city may be hampering him, and a little travel to work and back each day won't be too much trouble. The freedom represented by the summer card (Lughnasadh 11) could mean a change to what might have become a rather set way of life. The fresh country air and extra living space are suggested by the autumn card (Birca), which implies that Edward will love the apartment. He'll be lucky enough to get it if he wastes no time and acts now: accept new ideas. The winter card (Beltane 4) makes the message clear; tradition, of course, is the stately home itself. This is an encouragement to sit back occasionally and learn to enjoy the conventional pleasures of attractive, rich surroundings. This would not be a bad image for Edward, an up-and-coming young executive, and it would impress the outside world to see his modest car roll up the long, tree-lined drive to his small but grand country apartment! The answer is simple. Yes, go and see it. And please take it. Birca says so!

THE SUN WHEEL LAYOUT

T he Sun Wheel follows the course of the Sun through the year and relates to the Solar orb's visit to each of the zodiac signs. This will describe each month's events in the form of a calendar for the coming year. Following the traditional astrological sequence of the Sun's zodiac wheel on page 10, twelve cards are dealt, laid in a circle, turned over and read one by one. This sample reading for the coming year is for Lucy, a 30-year-old single mum with two small boys, Tom and Jack.

Lucy's Sun Wheel Reading

SPRING QUARTER: FEBRUARY, MARCH AND APRIL

FEBRUARY *Plans*
Imbolc 1 *Spontaneity*

Plans aren't something Lucy is good at. She'll never stop acting on impulse. Her star sign is Aquarius, one of the rulers of this card. She married young and divorced four years later. Lucy's responses are immediate and we'll expect February to reflect that. She'll make it up as she goes along.

MARCH *Challenge*
Rune 10 Nyd *Need, feeling the pinch*

Oh dear. It looks like this is going to be a lean month. Lucy is used to this and despite her slightly eccentric and haphazard Aquarian nature, she copes very well under duress. There could be money problems here though.

APRIL *Perseverance*
Beltane 8 *Protection*

There could be some help here after the previous month's setback. Lucy is very protective of her boys, and someone is probably going to devote the same kind of care to her. It wouldn't be a surprise to find her mother heeding the call as she has done a few times before.

SUMMER QUARTER: MAY, JUNE AND JULY

MAY *Confidence*
Rune 17 Tyr *Star, redressing the balance*

This card should inspire confidence. Stars always suggest hope and wishes coming true, so there will probably be some very good news this month.

JUNE *Love*
Beltane 2 *Appreciation*

OK, this card doesn't seem to suggest a new love affair as the June keyword implies. This is more about self-worth and Lucy feeling good about herself. She will value the work she puts into providing a pleasant and stimulating home for her sons and will enjoy the pleasure of being herself.

JULY *Feasting*
Beltane 9 *Celebration*

This card seems to show a family break that may even include Lucy's mum, as this card often refers to extended family as well as to celebration. The suggestion is certainly that Lucy, her mum, Tom and Jack may be in a position to take a well-earned holiday together. This is a good month!

AUTUMN QUARTER: AUGUST, SEPTEMBER AND OCTOBER

AUGUST *Maturity*
Imbolc 3 *Insight*

This suggests a contemplative time. August's keyword is 'maturity' and this will probably mean a great deal of serious thinking. It may well be that the previous month's break has inspired Lucy. Ideas that arise at this time are to be respected and worked on.

SEPTEMBER *Harvest*
Rune 14 Peorth *Gamble, fate, fortune*

Wow! Here in the position where we expect the year's harvest we have one of the major runes, Peorth. The keywords 'fate' and 'fortune' sound promising – has something of the previous month's 'insight' led to a little windfall?

OCTOBER *Resourcefulness*
Spring Equinox

Here we have the greenest of the Green Men – the Spring Equinox, which brings with it new beginnings. This indicates a very special month as the arrival of any of the four trump cards is cause for celebration. This card means that an opportunity or a second chance will be of great significance.

Winter Quarter: November, December and January

NOVEMBER *Preparation*
Imbolc 5 *Plans*

This card always indicates a very busy time, when the querent gets other people excited about their ideas. It also indicates ambitions being put firmly on the agenda. This is a key month for improving conditions for this small family.

DECEMBER *Rest*
Rune 1 Feoh *Cattle, wealth*

Feoh is the rune that describes material wealth that you can carry around. It doesn't only refer to money, it can be your talents as well. Feoh tells us that when we have come into possession of something good, we will be best off if we share it with others. This makes good sense and it may well be a significant month for Lucy's specific talents.

JANUARY *Renewal*
Lughnasadh 4 *Nourishment*

This looks like a month when Lucy could receive a little TLC in return for her previous self-sufficient efforts. Is there someone who would like to look after her? It's nice to be in a position to take a little after a year of giving.

FURTHER READING

Barrett, Clive *The Viking Gods*, The Aquarian Press, London, 1989

Blum, Ralph *The Book of Runes*, Connections Book Publishing, London, 2000

Cooper, Jason D. *Using the Runes,* The Aquarian Press, London, 1987

Dixon-Kennedy, Mike *Celtic Myth and Legend*, Blandford Press, London, 1997

Kemble, J. *Anglo-Saxon Runes*, Anglo-Saxon Books, Norfolk, 1991

Matthews, Caitlin *The Celtic Spirit*, Hodder and Stoughton, London, 1999

Matthews, John *The Celtic Shaman*, Element Books, London, 1992

Page, R.I. *An Introduction to English Runes,* Methuen, London, 1973

Paul, Jim (trans.) *The Rune Poem*, Chronicle Books, London, 1996

Pennick, Nigel *Runic Astrology,* Capall Bann Publishing, Berkshire, 1995

Peschel, Lisa *A Practical Guide to the Runes*, Llewellyn, St Paul, MN, 1988

ACKNOWLEDGEMENTS

To Ian Jackson for liking our synopsis and giving it the push required to make it a reality, Katie Ginn for tidying up the loose ends, Elaine Partington for waiting with unbelievable patience to see any art and text, and to Eddison Sadd for supporting this and our previous ventures and, above all, selling them.

EDDISON • SADD EDITIONS

EDITORIAL DIRECTOR	*Ian Jackson*
EDITOR	*Katie Ginn*
PROOFREADER	*Peter Kirkham*
ART DIRECTOR	*Elaine Partington*
MAC DESIGNER	*Brazzle Atkins*
PRODUCTION	*Sarah Rooney and Charles James*